Peeling the Onion:
Finding Out Who You Were Always Meant To Be

Dr. Cara DiMarco

All rights reserved.

Published by Inconvenient Women LLC

Peeling the Onion: Finding Out Who You Were Always Meant To Be

Copyright © 2015 Dr. Cara DiMarco

Cover art, book design, and illustration by Jessica Beaudet

Disclaimer: The following information is intended for general information purposes only. Individuals should always see their healthcare providers before administering any suggestions made in this book. Any application of the material set forth in the following pages is at the reader's discretion and is her or his sole responsibility.

No part of this publication may be reproduced, distributed, or transmitted in any form or by any means, including photocopying, recording, or other electronic or mechanical methods, without the prior written permission of the publisher, except in the case of brief quotations embodied in critical reviews and certain other noncommercial uses permitted by copyright law.

ISBN 1-51-776851-9

Printed by CreateSpace

Printed in the United States of America

First Edition: October 2015

Dedication

To all of the Women in Transition students who brought this book to life with their openness, courage and wisdom, especially the Life Transitions 2 women of Winter 2015, the WIT 1 women of Spring 2015 and the incredible staff of the Women's Program.

To Jessica Beaudet who fairy godmothered this book into being with her gorgeous artwork and generous willingness to grapple with the design of the book.

To Bob Lee who copy edited my first two books twenty years ago and showed up like a champ and made time to edit this manuscript with his keen eye for nuance and structure.

To all of the soulful healers and helpers that have helped me peel my own onion along the way: Vip Short, Rainey Taylor, Lyn Burg, Monica DeLuca, Kate Barry, Rich Freund, Megan Herring, Barbara Sullivan, Lee Daniel, Sabel Fleshman, Calvin Plantz, Mark Worthington, Mark Gunderson, Michelle Antico and dozens more.

And to Jake the rescue kitty who appeared in my life this summer and made my days of seclusion working on this book a delight by learning to fetch so that I could write and play with him simultaneously, reminding me that if a person is writing about being your truest, most flourishing self, playing and laughing must be interwoven along the way…

Contents

INTRODUCTION 9

CHAPTER 32: Be Your Own Fairy Godmother 13

CHAPTER 31: Blow Drying the Cat 19

CHAPTER 30: Bucket of Slugs 25

CHAPTER 29: Climbing Out of the Hamper 29

CHAPTER 28: Supergirl Underpants 33

CHAPTER 27: Playing Handball into the Drapes 39

CHAPTER 26: Telling Your Story 45

CHAPTER 25: Stop Waiting for Self-Worth 49

CHAPTER 24: Stinky Pants 53

CHAPTER 23: Learning To Trust 57

CHAPTER 22: Finding Your Light 63

CHAPTER 21: Brilliance Everywhere 67

CHAPTER 20: Carpet Angels 71

CHAPTER 19: Small Ears of Corn 75

CHAPTER 18: Sitting in Mud Puddles 79

CHAPTER 17: I Think I Can, I Think I Can, I Think I Can Stop Trying 85

Chapter 16: Infant Time   91

Chapter 15: Pineapple Upside Down Cake   95

Chapter 14: Don't Organize Around Chaos   99

Chapter 13: Cherish Yourself   103

Chapter 12: Don't Listen to the Birds in Your Head   107

Chapter 11: Create the Energy that is Missing   111

Chapter 10: Name it, Blame it, and Claim it   115

Chapter 9: The Solution is in the Middle   121

Chapter 8: Stop Trying to Make Others Stay   125

Chapter 7: Suspect the Best   129

Chapter 6: Four Steps to Making Your Dreams Come True   133

Chapter 5: Stop Waiting to Feel Motivated   137

Chapter 4: Claim Your Baggage   141

Chapter 3: Trying to Outrun Pain   145

Chapter 2: Trouble Saying No   149

Chapter 1: Fear Less Love More   153

Afterword   157

Peeling the Onion:
Finding Out Who You Were Always Meant To Be

Dr. Cara DiMarco

Introduction

I lost the outline for this book in 2000 and I'm not a person who loses things. I looked everywhere and once I became convinced that it was gone for good, I tried to recreate the outline. I couldn't recreate it and vowed to never again scribble my thoughts down on paper without making multiple copies.

Once I made peace with the fact that this book wasn't meant to be, I turned my focus to other projects. In 2009 I had a baffling array of physical symptoms that left me progressively weaker and struggling to walk even short distances. One doctor suggested that I might not have much time left and that I should think about what I wanted to do with my remaining time. The answer was a no-brainer. I wanted to keep doing the work I love with the amazing female students at the college and the female clients in my private psychology practice.

I decided to keep my medical condition private and channeled what little energy I had into helping women grow and flourish. Each evening after work, I'd sort through my files and boxes of paperwork, trying to winnow my belongings so that my sister would have less work to do after I passed away.

In early June of 2010, I had just sorted through another box and picked up a few sheets of newspaper dated years earlier and I became curious about what had happened in the news that day.

Peeling the Onion

As I unfolded the newspaper, guess what fluttered to the floor? My book outline from 2000 had reappeared.

Stunned, I stared in utter disbelief. I was positive it was lost for good, just as the doctors convinced me that my heath was lost for good. Clearly I was wrong about the outline because it was alive and well. What if the same could be true about my physical health? I decided to step away from Western medicine and turned to a homeopath in the hope that I could find my way back to health and together we started making some progress on my medical issues.

That being said, I was still aware that I might not be on the planet much longer. I decided that despite my physical weakness I was going to write this book. I'd write a page or two and then I'd have to nap. Soon doing even that became too exhausting. I found an old tape recorder in the back of a desk drawer, pulled it out and started dictating my book into the tape recorder.

As the summer progressed, so did the book. Years of students in the Women in Transition program had asked me to capture the principles I shared in class into a collection of short essays so that they could share them with their loved ones. I had resisted doing it because the majority of the stories were personal examples from my 20's and 30's on what *not to do* and the gradual insights that I had gained along the way. Did I really want the time I climbed into a wicker hamper captured forever in print? Or the time I unwittingly flashed my super girl underpants as a keynote speaker to a conference room full of people?

As I wrestled with my desire for privacy versus my desire to honor my students' request, I found a middle ground. I would use the book in a photocopied packet form as the unofficial textbook in the second level class in the Women in Transition program. So

Introduction

in fall of 2011, 60 women read these same pages and shared their questions and insights.

Each academic term, through the wisdom and clarity of these women, I was able to shape the book to increase its usefulness. One woman said "I think you should have people read it backwards from chapter 32 and end with chapter 1." Another woman said "It's like peeling an onion, taking off one layer after another of the behaviors, thoughts and ways of living that get in the way of us being our truest selves." A third woman said, "And when you work with onions in the kitchen, sometimes there are tears as you work your way toward the savory goodness that awaits at the end of the process." Wow! Can you see why I adore working with these women?

Flash forward to winter 2015 and a wonderful group of women in the program's second level class. We were a small group of 15 and our conversations were extraordinarily deep and emotionally rich. As the term drew to an end and we were evaluating the experience we had shared together, a woman spoke up and said, "You have to make this into a real book." I openly groaned and explained my ambivalence. She persisted and said, "There are so many women in communities that don't have this program and they need this information." The rest of the class chimed in with their agreement and that was the final push I needed.

Along the way, life and art imitated each other. As I was writing about peeling the onion, I was peeling the onion health-wise and went from profoundly unwell to being shockingly okay. So here I am and here is the book. Both of us somehow made it, despite all of the detours and us both getting lost along the way. And that's what this book is about: It's about all the ways that we as women get lost from our truest selves, the selves that can create lives worth living, worth longing for and worth actively moving toward, lives where we and those we love genuinely flourish.

Each short chapter is designed to peel back, one layer at a time, all the ways that our thoughts, emotions and behaviors have contributed to how we have gotten lost from who we were always meant to be: Our truest, most flourishing selves. Chapter by chapter, insight by insight, we find ourselves the same way we lost ourselves, one piece at a time.

When we start to find ourselves, piece-by-piece, we start to find our courage, the courage we thought we had lost. And when we find our courage, we become brave. We move from being stuck and begin to figure out what is true for us. We push past our fears and start to become who we were always meant to be: Women who flourish. And flourishing women create flourishing families and partners, flourishing workplaces and communities and this world deeply needs all of the flourishing energy that we can create.

I am excited to be on this journey with all of you and delighted that our insights can enrich each other. As you read through these pages, if you find that you have insights and 'aha' moments that you would like to share to be included in a future book, you can email me at peelingtheonion2015@gmail.com.

So let's begin this journey. Are you ready? Let's start peeling the onion…

CHAPTER 32

Be Your Own Fairy Godmother

Growing up as a young girl, did you ever wish for a fairy godmother to magically appear and wave her all-powerful wand, grant your deepest desires and chase away your fears? I know I did. And that wish persisted through childhood, followed me through numerous successes and achievements, through all kinds of growth and gains, all kinds of insights and inspirations. Throughout all of those moments I had a persistent wish for something bigger, better and bolder than myself to swoop down and transform everything into something magnificent.

I would have been at a loss back then to describe everything that magnificence would have encompassed, but I knew it had something to do with the insistent, internal voice I remember hearing even as a young child: "There's got to be something more." In those days, "something more" meant there had to be something beyond the abuse, the neglect and violence, beyond the ignorance, poverty and deliberate cruelty. There had to be a way to get to whatever was good, kind and loving in the world, a place where words soothed instead of stung, where touch was something to move toward not

Peeling the Onion

away from and where people loved instead of lashed out. I wanted a world of my own making, a world of goodness, of greatness, of gladness. I just wasn't certain how to get there.

Thus my long-standing wish for a fairy godmother. I figured that certainly she'd know how to get me to that place, or short of that, she could get me somewhere wonderfully neutral and safe. And once there, she could wave her wand and create all that I longed for and had always done without. So I kept my eyes open, kept looking for her, hoping she would appear in the slant of sunlight at the end of my bed, in the thick clump of cedar trees behind my house or the quiet corner of my school library. I kept hoping that she would come find me and help me on my way to a better life. Even though she never found me, or I never found her, the process of searching kept all of the beauty and lovely possibilities that she represented alive inside of me.

Flash forward to young adulthood where life, while greatly improved, still had not remotely reached my early visions of the magnificence possible through the powerful interventions of my still, yet to appear fairy godmother. I was still searching, still hungering for "something more," still hoping for some kind of outside change agent, some being or essence that would be capable of knowing, naming, creating and providing that elusive "something more." In an attempt to be helpful, my boyfriend in those long ago days, also a wonderful searcher him self, suggested that I take the personal growth seminar that he had just completed.

Always open to new information, I began attending the five-day seminar and felt I was learning many useful concepts and gaining helpful insights into myself. Still, I could not ignore the ever-present internal chant: "There's got to be something more." On the final day of the seminar, our closing exercise was a rebirthing visualization in which one of the seminar leaders guided us through envisioning the early moments and years of our lives. The experience contained many exceptionally powerful and evocative experiences for me, one of which I had at the very end of the exercise.

I saw a vision of myself at age four, standing in an enormous living room filled with wonderful mahogany furniture, deep green and burgundy velvet sofas and chairs, beautifully woven rugs and pillows, copper colored lamps that spread light throughout the room and tall shelves rich with books. In the far corner of the room, reaching from floor to ceiling was the most magnificently decorated Christmas tree I had ever seen with dozens and dozens of beautifully wrapped presents underneath. All of the presents were wrapped in glistening silver and gold foil paper, with huge glittery bows and shiny tags attached.

I watch my four-year-old self approach the tree and hear her think: "I wonder if one of those is for me?" Scared to look because what if the answer is no and scared to not look because what if the answer is yes, she stands still for a moment, barely breathing. She steadies her gaze, thinking: "Always better to know than not to know." My adult self smiles, witnessing the beginning of a motto that has served me well. My girl self moves closer to the packages, glances at the first tag, the second, the third, scans all of the presents under the tree. Each tag says the same thing: "To Cara, from Cara." They are all for me. They are all from me.

Stunned, my child self tries to breathe in what it means. All these gifts are mine. I can open them anytime I choose. Every day can be Christmas. I can give myself whatever I want. I did this: All of this beauty, all of this giving. This is the magnificence I have

Peeling the Onion

been waiting for, all that I have been wishing for all these years. I am my own fairy godmother.

In that moment, "something more" became "something mine." It became my own capacity and capability to create and grant myself whatever I most longed for in the world, from the largest manifestation of what I want the world to become to the smallest nuance of a feeling within me. I have the wand, the wisdom and the wherewithal to reduce the wounding I saw as a child and instead can increase the wellness and wonder experienced in the world. My adult self grabs that vision and runs with it. I envision gangs of happy, flourishing women stepping into their full fairy godmother nature, waving their magic wands wisely and well, creating better, brighter, bolder lives for themselves and those they love.

So dear fairy godmother of your own life, what would you like to do with your wand? What emotion, thought or way of being or believing do you most want to embody or weave into each day? More laughter? More curiosity? What small shift in your thinking would allow you to start seeing every day as a holiday of celebration? What gift, in the giving of it, would make you feel deeply glad each day? Love? Beauty? Kindness? Play? Hope? Humor? What makes you feel passionately alive? What do you want to create next in your life?

Will you join me? Be big, be bold and be brave in choosing experiences that bring deep gladness, energetic hope and active love into your life. Invite the best of everything straight into the center of your life, into all that you envision. Use your wand to create a stunningly beautiful life of your own choosing and your own making. You are both the gift and the giver of the gift. Be

Be Your Own Fairy Godmother

your own breathtaking, beautifully magnificent fairy godmother. Say yes. Say a big yes.

Note to myself:

What behaviors, thoughts and feelings am I willing to peel away and let go of to be my most flourishing self?

CHAPTER 31

Blow Drying the Cat

Pleasing others gets a bad name these days and women who regularly engage in pleasing others get labeled as being codependent, enabling, approval seeking, self-sacrificing or simply wimpy. Pleasing others certainly can be overdone and when it's taken to the extreme it can be very counterproductive and damaging. That being said, I'd like you to consider an entirely different notion of pleasing others in which pleasing does not mean displeasing, diminishing or damaging yourself. It is marvelous to please others and to love others in the ways they want to be loved. Just don't do it at the expense of your well-being and make certain that it comes from your joy of loving others well.

If loving others in ways they find pleasing and meaningful brings you joy, then you can feel confident that your giving is coming from a full, expansive and healthy place. If you are giving to get something (approval, attention, love) or to avoid losing something (security, affection, a relationship) then chances are your attempts to please others may create harm for you. This kind of pleasing has nothing to do with the joy of giving because that joy

Peeling the Onion

is nowhere in sight. Instead, fear and panic take center stage and drive this desperate giving. This is not true giving but is instead a dysfunctional swap meet where you offer up the core parts of your identity and well-being in exchange for what you fear you cannot live without.

Let me tell you what I learned about giving. It is not true giving if it radically subtracts from your well-being. It is not about giving pleasure and delight if it dismantles your strengths, your dreams, or your belief in your abilities and your self-esteem. It is not authentic giving if it causes you to pretend to be less than you are—less smart, less deserving, less clear, less capable and less true to what you think, feel, dream and desire in your life.

Please the people and creatures that sustain you because it delights you to be good to them. Give to others in the way they most love because you love doing it. This doesn't mean that what they love would be your first preference or that it even makes sense to you. As long as it brings them pleasure and doesn't diminish you, then give others what they love.

One of my favorite images for remembering this is recalling what Bob's cat Vinnie most loves to receive from me when I visit him. Vinnie is a gorgeous longhaired, white cat and like many white cats, he is absolutely deaf. Normal things that terrify other cats like vacuum cleaners fascinate Vinnie because he merely sees a large creature with a very long tail snaking across the carpet.

Now I had my own ideas about what might please Vinnie the most and my thoughts centered around things like catnip mice, a good ear rub or a nice piece of steamed chicken. While Vinnie certainly appreciated all of those offerings, you know what he loves the most? Vinnie likes to have me turn the blow dryer on cool and blow dry him from head to tail, from his ear tips to his tummy fur, for as long as my arm strength lasts. It would never have occurred to me to ever offer that to a cat as my cats run the moment I turn it on. Yet for Vinnie it's how he likes me to demonstrate my affection for him and while it seems totally wacky to me, I love to love him in the way he loves best—a full fluffing of his luxurious fur. Every time I visit, he lights up, makes a little "yippee" meow and runs to the bathroom where the blow dryer is located. I light up too, knowing that such a simple and silly thing will bring him so much pleasure.

It is that experience of lighting up within ourselves that provides an excellent gauge of whether we are giving and pleasing others in ways that do not disrupt our authenticity and well-being. Think about the ways you give to others. Do you light up at the thought of it? Do you feel dead, burdened or depressed? Do want to eat tons, sleep tons or snap other people's heads off after you've given in those ways? Even in the circumstances where you feel called to give because it is the right thing rather than the joyful thing to do, the giving should not damage or destroy any part of you. If it does, then that giving is not the right thing to do.

Also, stay away from people who don't want to give to you in the ways you most love, in the ways you feel most cared about and valued. A former boyfriend turned to me at a pivotal point in our relationship and said, "I'll give you what you want every once in awhile, provided you earn it." He anticipated that I would be blown away by his radical honesty. I, on the other hand, was blown away and horrified by his philosophy of me "earning" expressions of love and nurturing. And his assurance that what I wanted would occur "every once in awhile" sounded deliberately withholding,

Peeling the Onion

calculatingly miserly and offered odds no better than a slot machine located on the wrong side of town. It was horrifically discouraging to realize that standing before me was a man who took absolutely no pleasure in giving. None. Zippo. Zero.

Think about that for a moment: No pleasure in giving. I believe all the way down to my bone marrow that giving, pleasing and being good to others is supposed to be a delight. It is supposed to feel incredible, expansive, open-hearted, energizing and full of optimism in the belief that there is more than enough pleasure and joy to go around. We all know the difference. We know how incredible it feels when someone is happy in their role of giver, even if those experiences happened years ago.

I remember my grade school boyfriend Jon who delivered our newspaper and liked me because I was "smart, funny, cute and could kick the soccer ball over the school fence into the pig yard next door." The summer we were twelve we picked beans together and he kept putting his beans into my bucket. Despite my protestations for him to fill his own bucket, he continued to smile and put his beans into mine. When I asked him why, he simply said, "It makes me happy to see your bucket full." Now that was a boy who, even at age twelve, absolutely got the joy of pleasing others. It made him happy to see someone he loved have her bucket full.

Look for the people in your life that you love and cherish and whose buckets you want to fill. Give out of joy and gladness. Give in the ways that bring others and yourself the most pleasure and the peaceful knowledge that you are watching out for their well-being as well as your own. Put beans in someone's bucket. Fluff the cat on cool because he loves it and you love him loving it. Give because it

Blow Drying the Cat

feels good to give what others want and because generosity and love are amazingly renewable resources.

Recapture the pleasure a toddler has in giving someone a rock she has found or a piece of cookie. Give with the glee of knowing that you have something to give and the power to give it. Light up with true, healthy, happy giving—the kind of giving that just gets better and brighter. Give laughter. Give listening. Give seriousness and silliness. Give whatever fills someone's heart. Give in good, glad and glorious ways. Give those you love what they love in the ways you most love to give. Blow dry the cat.

Note to myself:

What behaviors, thoughts and feelings am I willing to peel away and let go of to be my most flourishing self?

Chapter 30

Bucket of Slugs

In the 1980's when I was a graduate student at the University of Oregon, I was invited to attend a workshop designed to prevent burnout in student leaders and high achievers. As I remember, the person presenting the information was a retired police detective from Seattle who had certainly experienced his own bouts of burnout and definitely knew his topic through first-hand experience.

Even though I've forgotten his name and much of what he said, the one thing that stuck with me was his "bucket of slugs" theory. As he explained it, all human beings (no matter how well or poorly adjusted) pack around a bucket of slugs. These slugs consist of whatever parts of ourselves we feel are inadequate, unacceptable and that we wish weren't true because we fear we will be rejected and unloved for possessing these traits.

So how do we handle the uncomfortable experience of dealing with our individual slug buckets? Typically what happens is that human nature kicks in and nearly everyone begins to look for a way to lighten their load by dishing their slugs into other people's buckets. This usually takes the form of the person looking

Peeling the Onion

for someone who is distracted and might not fully grasp what is happening as they are unwittingly taking on someone else's slugs.

People often say, "Don't take things so personally," and yet that comment so often follows an experience that is significantly hurtful and that feels incredibly personal. This is where the "bucket of slugs" theory is wonderfully helpful. What this theory says is that nearly everyone will (at least once in awhile) try to unload a slug on you, no matter how healthy they are or no matter how much they love you. Understanding this concept will allow you to view whatever slimy slug you just received as an unfortunate aspect of human nature—that we all seek to find relief from pain and discomfort by dishing off our slugs on others. Instead of feeling deliberately persecuted when someone slips you a slug, you can change your perspective. You can realize that it may have far more to do with the simple fact that you were closest in proximity or seemed to have room in your bucket than stemming from any personal, intentional assault upon your self-worth or well-being.

Instead of lashing out at the person who hurt you or retaliating by flinging some of your slugs in their direction, you can simply and non-reactively fish their slugs out of your bucket, read their name tags and calmly send them back to their true owners. Taking this perspective allows you the opportunity to not take offense at other people's unkind behavior. By doing this you can notice what is unacceptable, name it out loud and return whatever is negative to its original owner.

It is vital in this process that you trust what you know to be true about your authentic self. Believe your truth. Being self-questioning and introspective is extremely healthy. It is wonderful to ask: How may I be contributing to what I am experiencing?

What isn't especially healthy is moving from self-questioning into agonizing self-doubt. Self-doubt only diminishes your strength. It does not increase your resiliency, openness, creativity or your courage. It leads to greater fear, constriction and emotional limitations. It makes all forms of flourishing nearly impossible.

It is so important to remember all the things that you know are true about yourself when you are faced with the challenging task or sorting out whether a slug belongs to you or to someone else. Ask others you trust for their input and ideas, but don't hand out scorecards that rate your worth to anyone. If you do that, then you'll start to shape your responses around not losing approval rather than increasing your accurate perception of your authentic self. It's okay to be lost and confused through the slug bucket sorting process. Just remember that you don't have to wait for full wisdom to arrive before you take some beginning actions in your life. You don't need to know everything before you begin or before you start heading in the direction that you sense is right. Wisdom is the payoff farther down the road for a well-lived life.

Trust what you know. Name your sturdiness. Flex your strength. Say what is true for you. Define yourself on your own terms. Stop trying to get everyone to like and approve of you. Even if you were successful at such an impossible task, you don't have time for everyone to like you because they would all want to be your friend. Accept and approve of your authentic self. Don't take on other people's slugs. Check the nametags and if they belong somewhere else, just send them and the negativity back to where it truly belongs.

Peeling the Onion

Note to myself:

What behaviors, thoughts and feelings am I willing to peel away and let go of to be my most flourishing self?

CHAPTER 29

Climbing Out of the Hamper

We've all had points in our lives where we have, consciously or unconsciously, maneuvered ourselves into particularly low circumstances emotionally, mentally and physically. As depleting as these events may be to our energy and self-esteem, I believe that it is precisely in these moments when we may be the most profoundly open to delving into new insights and ways of conducting our lives.

My personal pinnacle of pathetic behavior occurred in the 1980's, mercifully decades ago. I was in college, dating a young man who professed monogamy and undying love. He often traveled out of town and had given me a key to his apartment, which was larger and quieter than mine, so that I could come over and study in comfort while he was away.

One rainy Friday night when he was supposedly out of town, I was at his apartment, sitting at his breakfast bar with my books spread across the counter top, studying for exams. Somewhere into my third hour of studying, I heard loud footsteps, drunken laughter and two voices singing their way up the stairs to my boyfriend's apartment. As they approached the front door, I realized it was the

Peeling the Onion

voice of my boyfriend and a female neighbor of his who deliberately "forgot" my name each time she saw me and would say, "Hi Carita," and look me up and down as though I was a huge fashion misstatement.

Now the natural, healthy and appropriate response would have been to remain seated at the breakfast bar with my textbooks and simply hold my ground physically and emotionally, especially given the fact that he had given me permission to be in his apartment anytime he was out of town. So did I do that? Unfortunately that option did not even remotely occur to me until much later.

Instead, I panicked and totally lacking even a speck of assertiveness and internal fortitude, I grabbed my books, stuffed them in the cupboard beneath the breakfast bar and then ran down the hall. As the front door was opening, I panicked even further, dashed into the bathroom and then realized I couldn't exit the bathroom without them seeing me.

Now at this moment I could have still turned the situation around by flushing the toilet, washing my hands and walking out of the bathroom. Doing that would have, however, required that I felt like I belonged there and had a right to take up space, be inconvenient, rock the boat, claim what was mine but I still did not believe those things were true for me. So I did the only thing my self-esteem at the time allowed: I looked for a place to hide and the only place available was his clothes hamper. So I climbed into the hamper.

His hamper was one of those round, straw-colored, roughly-woven baskets with a matching round lid that was common in the 1980's. The two positive things about the hamper were that the loose weaving provided a bit of air circulation and a limited view of the bedroom diagonally across the hall. Other than that, there I was, cramped and squatting in his sweaty workout clothes wondering exactly how I had come to be in this sorry predicament and exactly how I was going to extricate myself.

Suffice it say, it went from horrid to unspeakable with the two of them proceeding to drunkenly fumble on the bed, while my soon-to-be ex-boyfriend reassured her that I was "no one important" in his life and that he was just "trying to be kind" by spending time with me. My heart froze upon hearing this and my head reeled with the absurdity of climbing into the hamper to avoid an awkward moment with a man who clearly did not value me.

Mercifully, they stopped rolling around and decided to leave to get a bite to eat. Once I was certain that they were gone, I climbed out of the hamper, washed my hands and face and looked long and hard at my reflection in the mirror. It was in that moment that I decided I had to change my apologetic stance toward life, my belief that if my presence would create discomfort, then I should disappear and be absolutely invisible, be neither seen nor heard. It was also then that I decided that while I could not control whether someone chose to value me, I could consciously and consistently choose to value myself by standing up for my right to claim the best of my partner's honesty and integrity.

What I also learned is that hiding from what you fear never creates protection or safety. As uncomfortable as confrontation might be, it is often the willingness and courage to face the confrontation that brings the truth into full view. And it is in the full seeing and hearing of the truth that we are in the most powerful position possible to take care of our hearts and sense of well-being.

Peeling the Onion

Be brave. Be strong enough to dare to see what is true. Face what actually exists, not what you wish was true. Step up to what you fear. Walk right up to it, poke it in the chest, and stare it in the eye. Hold your ground. Don't flee what you need to face, because while the truth may hurt, it is running from the truth that creates the harm. You can survive whatever you discover. Stand still. Simply see what is true. You can triumph over whatever you let yourself know. Let the truth in. Climb out of the hamper.

Note to myself:

What behaviors, thoughts and feelings am I willing to peel away and let go of to be my most flourishing self?

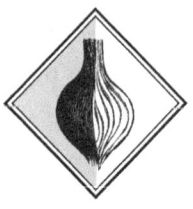

Chapter 28

Supergirl Underpants

Women. Power. Women and power. What a loaded topic for most women, even for those of us that embrace and actively seek opportunities for the healthy expression of our power. The conflicts we can feel over the possession and expression of power are seemingly endless. Is it okay to have power? If so, how much, in what areas, in what ways? Why does expressing our power, being visible in our power feel so vulnerable and risky? Can we have both love and power or does one cancel out the other? And the questions go on and on…

As a young girl I was always fascinated by the idea of someone having super human powers that they could use to smite anything harmful to humankind. I especially loved Wonder Woman with her magic bracelets that she would strike together to unfurl her power in the name of all that was right and good. I was so taken with those bracelets that I constructed my own out of empty cardboard toilet paper tubes, masking tape and tin foil. I would run around the house with my power bracelets on and screech to a halt in front of any wrongdoing, strike my bracelets together and race on to where the world next needed my super powers.

Peeling the Onion

Shortly after that, I somehow learned that Superwoman (who I also thought was amazing) had a sidekick named Supergirl. Supergirl's name was Kara, the same as mine, just a different spelling.

This was a dream come true for me, because as a young girl I didn't know another soul with my name and while I loved my name, I often wished I knew one other person who shared it with me. I was ecstatic. I tied a doll blanket around my neck and continued running around with my power bracelets on. Anytime someone would ask me who I was, I would say: "I am Supergirl and my name is Cara."

I loved my power then, loved to use it in the service of all that was good. I loved to use it to protect my beloved cat from barking dogs, felt courageous using it to convince my baby sister that nothing could hurt us in the middle of the night. I had my power bracelets on and knew how to use them to keep anything bad or frightening from destroying us.

Flash forward to young adulthood where I had learned many unfortunate lessons regarding the desirability of my power. I learned my power was unattractive, unfeminine, and far too intense and would leave me, in my father's words "a bitter and lonely woman." So I tried to dim my power, tried to be less strong, less able, less brave, less clear and less certain. While I definitely diminished my self-esteem, I still continued to have success and impact in the world, but the only difference was I felt deeply unsure of myself and somehow perpetually apologetic and wrong.

These feelings were at an all time peak at the point in my life where I was to give one of my first presentations at a professional conference. One of my friends who knew me from my early Supergirl days realized how apprehensive I was feeling and as a sign of support, purchased a pair of white cotton Supergirl underpants for me. These were a full-fledged grownup version of what you would imagine an eight-year-old girl's super hero underwear would look like, white cotton briefs with brightly colored supergirls flying in all directions.

Well, I wore them to my presentation under nicely tailored black dress pants. My presentation was to extend from mid-morning to mid-afternoon, with brief breaks in the morning and afternoon and a lunch social hour. I had enormous self-doubt regarding my ability to contribute anything useful for the full length of the program. After all, what did I really know? What if it was wrong? Who would want to listen to it anyway? Not exactly an internal dialogue destined to create success.

Despite being terrified that I would bore them senseless, I showed up on the morning of the conference and began my presentation and made it to the morning break without putting anyone to sleep. Deeply relieved, I went to use the bathroom, washed my hands, checked my makeup and felt reasonably ready to push on with my topic until lunch.

As I resumed my presentation, I began to feel the group become more focused and they seemed to be more intensely connected with my words and gestures as I moved back and forth from behind the podium to walk across the elevated speaker's platform. This continued as the clock ticked its way toward the lunch hour and I began to feel this small glow inside as I realized I must be saying something useful and reaching them in important, dynamic ways.

Nice thought. The truth was that (as I realized when I went to wash my hands right before lunch) I had left my pants unzipped since the morning break and much of the rapt attention stemmed

Peeling the Onion

from audience members trying to figure out what was emblazoned all over my enormous white cotton briefs.

I was horrified and had there been a bathroom window wide enough to crawl through, I would have slid down the side of the building and slunk out of town, never to be heard from again. Since that wasn't an option, I had no idea what on earth I was going to do when I resumed speaking after lunch. Trying to pretend I hadn't been walking around with my super hero underwear flashing the room all morning seemed pathetic and absurd, yet deliberately bringing it up and creating more attention seemed awkward and humiliating.

In all of my misery in that moment, I learned an incredibly important lesson. Because I had no clue how to handle the situation, no map of the right thing to do, I decided to go with my gut, with my intuition. And what it told me was: Be real. So that's what I did. I walked back up to the speaker's platform after lunch and said, "How many of you noticed that my pants were unzipped for an hour and a half?" The crowd started laughing and everyone put up their hands. I then said, "And here I was thinking that you were all fully fascinated by what I had to say but you were really trying to figure out what was on my underwear." More laughter, more head nods.

What was most ironic for me was that the next topic I was to present was on the topic of authentic power, how we as women lose our power and what we can do to reclaim it. It was the topic that I felt the most ill at ease about, fraudulent talking about a process that I didn't understand myself. And yet, the supergirl underpants came to the rescue.

Supergirl Underpants

Following my intuition, I did one of my first public disclosures about my past, sharing my young supergirl heroics, complete with power bracelets. The presentation soon became a discussion of all the moments of magnificence and power we remembered as young girls and when we, as one woman so beautifully phrased it, "decided to take off our bracelets and hide them away."

We shared about our longing to experience again those early heroic moments, full of daring and doing, full of the power to impact and change all the things that create loss and pain in the world. We talked about creating a new notion of power, not power over others, not power to dominate, demean or damage. We talked about power over ourselves, power to dream our destiny into reality, power to create a heroic life where the very best of us is used in full service to the world.

One woman spoke up and said, "We need to make power bracelets right now so we always remember this moment." Someone dashed to the hotel kitchen and another to the conference office and soon our supplies were assembled. Envision if you will, 150 women dressed in business suits laughing as they constructed their power bracelets and helped one another fasten them to their wrists.

Soon we were standing in small circles. I asked each woman to claim the power she wanted to harness in her life, naming as many forms of power that she wanted and to strike her bracelets as she named each one. Women throughout the room were laughing, crying, whooping, clapping as each woman stepped into her own heroic moment, made her power real, visible, made her power proudly and joyfully hers. When each woman had taken her turn, I asked them each to take a solemn vow that each of us in the room will always strive to use our power for good, to use our power to

Peeling the Onion

uplift, to inspire, to sustain, to soothe, to share the best of what we know and see with one another.

Use your power to create whatever matters most to you. Use it to love well and live well. Use it to turn hurt into healing, to turn criticism into compassion and to turn fear into faith. Find your bracelets, find your bravery and find your belief in your own power, spectacularly used in the service of all that is good. Go find it wherever you left it and bring it back. We so desperately need the best of your power. And when you find it, tell us all about it. Share your heroic self out loud and strike your power bracelets together. The world is full of Supergirls. They are everywhere. I have met them. And you are one.

Note to myself:

What behaviors, thoughts and feelings am I willing to peel away and let go of to be my most flourishing self?

CHAPTER 27

Playing Handball into the Drapes

Every day, hundreds of times a day, we have the choice to determine where we send and how we use our energy. We can decide to send our energy towards situations and individuals where we get to have a mutual and positive impact. We can send our energy into circumstances and people where nothing that we do, from our finest moments to our foulest ones, creates any impact on the situation. I call this playing handball into the drapes.

Even if you've never actually played handball, you probably still know that a vital component in the game of handball is that you need a solid wall to act as an adequate playing surface. One of the major points of handball is that the force of your arm impacts the force of the ball, which in turn impacts the force of the ball striking the wall and the force of the ball as it comes back to you.

In other words, the energy you expend and the intensity you utilize shapes some of what happens next. However, this is not true when it comes to playing handball into the drapes. Unfortunately, some individuals in the world conduct themselves like a large set of very heavy, very dense living room drapes. No matter what

Peeling the Onion

wonderful, authentic, high energy, positive things you send their way, everything still strikes the dead, flat energy of these people's inner emotional drapes. This can cause the very best of you to either have zero impact or even worse, a negative impact that leaves you feeling that you are less than you were before you sent your energy toward them.

For me, the metaphor of remembering to not play handball into the drapes is about being willing to always ask myself: Is this a wise use of my time and energy? Sometimes in the process of loving people who are fully deserving of our love it is necessary to go through difficult times as we renegotiate our way to deeper, more vulnerable levels of loving and allowing ourselves to be loved. I believe that this kind of struggle is a wise use of our time.

The struggle that is not a wise use of our time is when we hurt for no growth-based reason. Instead of the temporary discomfort and hurt leading to future depth and intimacy with others, the pain instead becomes ongoing, resulting in devastating despair over trying, over and over again, despite the fact that we are getting nowhere with our efforts.

Growing pains are definitely okay and absolutely necessary for our well-being. What is not okay is to have the kind of pain that leads to disabling depression and inertia. You need to get sick of that pain, grow past it and get rid of it. If it hurts and the love doesn't substantially outweigh the heartache, then it is time to stop no matter how strong the drive is to keep on trying.

It is emotionally dangerous and futile to attempt to love people who are afraid of contact, afraid of realness, afraid of feeling the importance and impact of you in their life. No matter how much you love someone, they still need to offer you something that is

Playing Handball into the Drapes

powerful, profound and lasting besides the intensity and repercussions of their wounds.

It is incredibly important to remember as you are trying to extricate yourself from playing handball into the drapes that everything you see and experience that is not comprised of love and positive intention is instead comprised of fear and pain. When others are deeply wounded and unable or unwilling to take the steps to heal themselves, their only power comes through withholding what others want or finding other damaging ways to disrupt, dismantle or destroy the best in those they profess to love.

People who are living their lives from a drape perspective are not interested in adding to or enhancing the positive energy in your life. This is why they send their most powerful and focused energy into working to discern what is most vital to you and then systematically and cruelly withhold the very things you desire. Remember this: Individuals who live their lives from a drapes perspective only have power over you as long as you are struggling to get what is being withheld.

If you are like most people and you've been struggling, striving and agonizing for a long time over what is being withheld, you've most likely been far too busy and exhausted to see how incredibly little that person offers you. In other words, while the longing in you may be enormous and absolutely genuine, what the person who chooses to withhold has is usually microscopic, incredibly inconsistent and much more about pretending to possess what you desire rather than actually having it.

It is absolutely normal to want someone you love to love you back or to want someone you give to thoughtfully and generously to return the same, but when the expenditure of the best of your

Peeling the Onion

energy only brings defeat and deadness, it is time to recognize that you are playing handball into the drapes. With this recognition, it is imperative that you find a way to stop doing what is futile and has no future, except a future that will continue to create unnecessary loss and pain. Even if you can't find the willingness or desire to walk away, walk away anyway and trust that your decision will begin to feel right as the pain begins to disappear.

Stop fighting to get what is being withheld. If it's not being freely offered and the person is trying to keep you hooked into their life, they are not interested in you and your well-being. Compassionate people who can't or who choose not to give you what you want will tell you that and lovingly exit your life. Emotionally dangerous, playing handball-into-the-drapes people will tell you they aren't giving it to you because you don't deserve it yet or you keep doing things wrong and then they will tell you that they keep you in their life because they love you. Don't believe them. These individuals will take your heart hostage until your usefulness has expired and then you are discarded.

Don't use the best of yourself trying to prevent the inevitable. Put an expiration date on your interaction with that person and take a deep breath and leave. No matter how horrible it feels in the moment, it will be so much shorter in duration than the length of pain you will experience trying to get someone who withholds love to freely offer it to you. There are better places for you to be and better people for you to meet and love.

Let go of what hurts and what doesn't work. When someone withholds what you no longer want, they go from holding a bag of priceless gems to holding a bag of dog poop. What if you can get what you want without all the unnecessary pain? It really can

Playing Handball into the Drapes

happen. Stop doing what doesn't make sense. Stop playing handball into the drapes.

Note to myself:

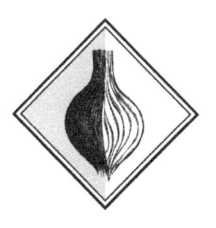

What behaviors, thoughts and feelings am I willing to peel away and let go of to be my most flourishing self?

CHAPTER 26

Telling Your Story

A lot of people tell me their stories. While I know that people have happy stories and stories of laughter and hope, the stories I usually hear are stories of pain and loss, of betrayal and abandonment, abuse and neglect, terror and touch that only harmed and never held. They are often stories of anguish and regret, longing, bewilderment and despair over love that has left their lives.

As truly tragic as many of those stories are, what is even more devastating is how people are often held hostage as adults by the bad storylines inflicted upon them as children. These bad storylines continue to keep ancient untruths alive: You'll always be alone, no one will ever love you, you'll never amount to anything, you're not _____ (pretty enough, smart enough, happy enough). These bad storylines scare people out of living rich and fulfilling lives because they feel defeated before they begin, because everything seems too hard, too much to consider or somehow possible for others but impossible for them.

I am a big believer in people telling their stories of what has terrified and wounded them as many times as they need to and

Peeling the Onion

turning the story this way and that way, shining a light in every shadowy corner, turning it upside down and shaking every piece loose, spreading every micro-bit on the table and sorting through each piece and making sense out of the senseless and inexcusable events. Yet it is vital that the process doesn't stop there. Once the story has been reasonably well unearthed and analyzed, it is absolutely crucial to start seeing the story differently.

By differently, I don't mean pretending that whatever happened didn't happen or didn't have whatever impact it did on you. What I am referring to is looking at the purpose of continuing to tell your story after you've explored all the angles and edges of it. It's absolutely okay to continue telling your story to yourself and others, however it's vital that you ask yourself this: Are you telling your story as a way to explain why you are stuck, as a reason for why you are scared or not up to the task before you? Are you telling your story as an excuse to stay mired and not challenge yourself to change and grow or as a way to get others to realize why they shouldn't expect whatever they are expecting from you?

Don't use your story as a reason to stay stuck in all the old limitations and fears. You are bigger, better and more capable than that and you deserve an opportunity to have a different experience. Tell your story as a way of moving yourself forward. Tell your story to motivate yourself to pursue something more than what you have survived. Tell your story to make something amazingly purposeful and positive out of every bad thing that happened to you.

Tell your story as a way to remind yourself of how far you have come and how far you are going and to help others see their way out as well. Tell your story to remain clear about what you are never returning to again, what you will no longer allow, what negative

Telling Your Story

things you know are not the truth nor the totality of you. Tell your story until you have absolute clarity that it is exactly that and only that—it is only the story of what happened to you and it never has been (nor ever will be) the essence and truth of all that you are or will grow to be as your life unfolds.

And when you feel ready, then and only then, try telling yourself a new story, a story rooted in the here-and-now and expanding into the future, populated by loving people, kind experiences, appropriate challenges, consistent support and all of the things that you find inviting and rewarding.

Stop scaring yourself by continuing to repeat everything bad that has happened and that you worry will continue to happen in your life. Give yourself a new storyline from this point forward. Find the happy ending waiting inside of you and start envisioning and verbalizing it. Start creating the happy ending you've always longed for and start living the life that will move you toward your happy ending.

Start by telling yourself and others that new story. Breathe it in. Laugh hard and loud at your favorite parts. Sit on the edge of your chair and let your eyes grow big as you talk about how incredible it was when you first felt how much love, joy, hope and happiness was waiting for you.

List all the moments of magnificence you want to come true for you, all the ways you want to love and be loved, all the ways you want to know that being here made a difference, made an impact, left the world braver, better and more beautiful. Find a story that you love, one that moves you and one that you can't put down. Make that the story you tell. Make that the story that comes true. Start moving toward your happy ending.

Peeling the Onion

Note to myself:

What behaviors, thoughts and feelings am I willing to peel away and let go of to be my most flourishing self?

CHAPTER 25

Stop Waiting for Self-Worth

How often in life do you postpone doing the things you are drawn to and know would enrich your life? What holds you back from the things you love? What do you tell yourself that prevents you from moving toward what you desire?

If you are like many of the women that I have had the honor of working with, this stuck-ness and inertia have their roots in the belief that you are not worthy of having what you desire and that you have no right to move toward what you hunger for until you have done enough worthwhile behaviors to earn what you desire. Isn't that a mean, harsh and punitive way to live? Have you ever noticed that no matter how hard you may work to prove your worth that it always seems that you fall short and the standard keeps being raised?

Why is it that we often can encourage other women and support them pursuing the things that spark and enliven them, but find it so difficult to allow ourselves the same freedom and open wanting of what we desire in our lives? Why do we give ourselves so many conditions regarding when we can begin, assuming we let

Peeling the Onion

our selves begin at all? Why is it always framed around after the kids are grown, or after your partner's promotion or your friend's divorce? All of this essentially says the same thing: After I have fully and successfully cared for everyone else, then and only then can I consider that I might be worthy of the same care and focused energy that I extend to others.

What if all of a sudden you just decided that you were worth the best of your own energy, the best of your attention and interest, the best of your encouragement and enthusiasm? What if you simply told yourself that it was smart to let yourself explore what you are curious about and pursue what you are passionate about? What if you chose to give yourself experiences that helped you truly flourish? What if you decided that it was a good investment to help yourself flourish whether or not you felt worthy enough to flourish? Wouldn't that be a radically different way of living?

Can you imagine beginning each day by allowing yourself to seek out experiences that bring you aliveness and joy? What if, instead of listening to the internal and sometimes external voices that say, "That's selfish," you just ignored those voices and told yourself, "It's always a good investment to move toward joy" and just did it, whether or not you fully believed it?

What if you kept on moving toward the things that inspire joy and aliveness in you, continued telling yourself "It's a good investment" and kept on doing it even when you weren't fully convinced? You know what will eventually happen? You will believe it because all those acts of taking your self-worth on faith rather than waiting for the feeling of self-worth to spontaneously arise will have allowed you to take action on creating a life where the woman you were always meant to be can begin to unfold and blossom.

Stop Waiting for Self-Worth

You may have no clue where that woman is because she has been missing-in-action for so long. Or you may feel that you've never seen her before because she's never had a chance to exist. Fair enough and certainly true enough. And yet I have an idea of who she is for I've seen her glimmer around the edges of thousands of pairs of women's eyes. I've seen her shine when she finally sees and celebrates the parts of her that have gone deeply unrecognized, unvalued and unloved for years.

I've seen her glow and grow in all kinds of gloriously unexpected and endless ways when she comprehends that she doesn't have to live her life looking for an unending stream of approval. I've seen her change her life when she starts to understand that if too many people think too well of her all of the time, then perhaps she isn't living in a way that truly causes her to feel well and welcome in her own life.

Once you start creating a life that feels truly worth living rather than just enduring, then you will begin to encounter increasing evidence of your self-worth. You have the capability to do this right now, right this minute. You don't have to look good or feel good about yourself to be able to take action and make this change.

Stop looking for your worth in other people's eyes or in their applause or approval. If you want people to like you, fine go for it, knock yourself out. But promise me this, don't ever again confuse whether they like you with whether you are worth anything because they have nothing to do with each other.

Live the life you would live if you thought you were incredible. Take on the challenges you'd dare to tackle if you thought you were amazing. Love big and bold, the way you would if you knew you were absolutely and unarguably lovable.

Peeling the Onion

Because you know what? You are all that and more. You are incredible. Amazing. Lovable. Powerful. Clear. Deserving of a life that inspires you, intrigues you, invigorates you. Let yourself off the hook. Whatever you did that wasn't wonderful probably doesn't merit a life sentence of deadness, deprivation and drudgery. You still deserve joy. Trust that you are worth it. Open the door and go find the life you love.

Note to myself:

What behaviors, thoughts and feelings am I willing to peel away and let go of to be my most flourishing self?

CHAPTER 24

Stinky Pants

One of the biggest mistakes that we make as women is when we beat ourselves up over perceived or real mistakes. While I certainly believe that it is essential for us to be introspective and explore what went wrong and what we'd do differently next time, it makes no sense that we berate ourselves for mistakes.

If the point is to learn from mistakes so we can be more successful in the future, then beating ourselves up is counterproductive. Who actually feels open to learning when they are being yelled at and criticized for every less-than-perfect choice they've made from first grade forward? No one learns anything well or lasting in an atmosphere of harsh criticism, yet that is precisely the tone of most women's self talk: "That was so stupid," or "That was even more pathetic than usual," or "When will you ever learn?" None of this has ever inspired anyone to do anything brighter, anything better or anything braver. It is a horrible morale and spirit breaker and it never works as a motivator, except for women to feel worse about themselves. And more importantly, it's an incredibly mean way to treat yourself.

Peeling the Onion

One crucial step out of the trap of treating ourselves in harsh and unkind ways is to grant ourselves some grace and compassion regarding what we feel we should have known before all of the vital knowledge was available to us. I wish I could say that I learned this on my own, but the truth is that I learned the best lesson ever on how to view mistakes from a three-year-old girl who intuitively knew how to trust herself and the unfolding nature of life.

It was late summer and Claire, my amazing three-year-old neighbor girl was sitting on the front steps of her house with a scrunched-up expression on her face. I stopped and asked, "Claire honey, what's wrong?" She answered that a neighbor boy her age had been visiting her in her wading pool and that he "started farting and farting and farting." I responded, "No wonder your face is all scrunched-up. What did you do then?" With a very serious look on her face she answered: "I sent him home."

I then sat down next to her on the steps and we sat in silence together for a few minutes. Claire looked over at me, tilted her head and said, "You know what Cara? Sometimes you can't tell who is going to have stinky pants until you've been around them for awhile." So simple, yet so brilliant.

I sat there with my mouth open, absolutely speechless in the face of her three-year-old wisdom and clarity. She wasn't beating herself up for not knowing and predicting his behavior in advance. She wasn't saying, "What is it about me that attracts boys who do these sorts of things?" She didn't obsess about whether she had done or said something that caused his behavior or whether that made it her fault. She also didn't guilt trip herself into tolerating unacceptable behavior by telling herself, "I should be more understanding and loving. He probably had a bad childhood or fought with his mom." Instead, she decided that his behavior wasn't okay. She didn't feel the need to teach or guide him to engage in appropriate, non-farting behavior. Instead, she simply sent him home.

Even more powerful was her awareness that you can't always know who is going to have stinky pants when you first meet them. Sometimes you have to be around someone for a long time to finally see the true essence of who they are. I suppose you could beat yourself up for not being all-knowing but that seems pretty unreasonable given the fact that truly knowing the character of a person is a process that generally happens over time.

Sometimes people's stinky pants will be apparent immediately. Other times it will take longer to recognize it. You're not stupid, blind or pathetic because you didn't spot the truth sooner. Instead of being mean to yourself because you didn't realize it earlier, give yourself acknowledgement that you understand what is true now.

Trust that the reason that you know the truth now is because the time is right for you to know it, see it and be able to take appropriate action. Remember that it often takes time and experience to see deeply and well into another person. Sometimes you will be wonderfully delighted to uncover increasingly rich, truly lovely layers of a person's character. Other times that uncovering will reveal someone's gigantic stinky pants.

When that happens, don't blame yourself. Instead, thank yourself for being able to see the truth, for being brave enough to not have to pretend that someone is something that they're not just to not have to be alone. Don't tear down your perceptions, your intelligence or your intuition. Build yourself up by believing in yourself and your ability to powerfully act on the truth. Follow

Peeling the Onion

Claire's incredibly clear and healthy advice: If someone has stinky pants, get them out of your wading pool and send them home.

Note to myself:

What behaviors, thoughts and feelings am I willing to peel away and let go of to be my most flourishing self?

CHAPTER 23

Learning to Trust

One of the most difficult life tasks that many of us face is learning how to truly trust—openly, wisely and well. How do you decide whom to trust, what to trust, when to trust? Have you given up on trusting because you feel like you always get hurt? Are you willing to trust provided you can just figure out the right way to do it? Would you like to know how? Okay, here goes: All sturdy, reliable and sensible trust comes with finding the trustworthiness within yourself rather than looking for the trustworthiness in others. I always wanted there to be some external formula that once I understood it and committed it to memory, it would guarantee that I would always choose the right people and experiences. Despite all of my efforts, I finally realized that there wasn't anything that could do that for me. And believe me, I searched for it.

I know that isn't good news, I can hear the groans of my women students and still remember mine when I first realized that there was no solid way to form a sense of trust if it was only based on how others behaved or how situations turned out. It felt like so many of those other seemingly unsatisfying solutions to complex dilemmas

Peeling the Onion

like all love begins with self love, or weight loss occurs when you decrease calories and increase exercise. It's all so clearly true, yet simultaneously so unappealing because it means that in order to change whatever is creating discomfort and dissatisfaction for us, we have to change things within ourselves rather than things outside of ourselves.

So often the impulse is to look outside of yourself and say, "I know there are trustworthy people out there, I just need to figure out how to spot them." And while it's true that some people are far more worthy of your trust than others, how do you know for certain that someone is truly trustworthy? Isn't a trustworthy person someone who hasn't broken your trust and has thus far behaved in trustworthy ways?

So then how can you fully relax into a sense of trust if that all can be taken away in one significant untrustworthy act? Do you spend the rest of your life being vigilant, watching for any sign that someone is going to deceive or hurt you? Do you pounce on any inconsistent behavior or comment, looking for ways in which you are going to be misled and do you question and accuse others of having harmful intentions toward you? Do you keep yourself so defended and distanced from others that you don't allow anyone far enough into your life to have even a chance to betray you?

There are no good answers when you try to locate your sense of trust and safety in things outside of yourself. This concept was forever driven home for me when I met a woman in her seventies who just had her husband of 52 years report that he was leaving her because he had decided that he didn't want to be married anymore. Everyone who knew him was shocked, including his

Learning to Trust

soon-to-be-ex-wife, because he had always seemed to be a happy and loving husband.

I was fortunate enough to get to watch this amazing woman's process as she moved from despair over the loss of her marriage, to determination to not let that loss define her safety and sense of trust in herself and in the world. A year after her heartbreaking loss, I asked her how she made her way from all the tears and torment to the place of triumph that she now occupied.

She smiled and was quiet for a moment. Then she shared two important insights with me. The first was that she promised herself that no matter what had happened, no matter how hurt and lost she felt, she was not going to stop believing in what was good, kind and right in the world. She decided that just because he broke her trust in him that didn't mean that he broke her ability to trust herself and her belief in all that was good in the world.

Second, she decided that every time she felt scared at facing a new task or emotional challenge, that instead of feeling depressed or throwing her hands up and saying, "This is too hard," she would instead say, "How can I learn this now?" Every time her fear would resurface, she would shift her focus from the fear and tell herself, "Just don't go anywhere but straight into this one question: How can I learn this now?"

Think about what would happen if we did that with the task of learning to trust. What if we decided to trust that no matter what life brings, no matter how difficult or painful an experience might be, that we could trust ourselves to either know how to handle it or trust ourselves to learn whatever we need to know to eventually handle it?

Peeling the Onion

Do you see how that shifts the focus? If you trust your ability to persevere and learn what you need to make your life work well, then everything else falls away—all the attempted mind reading of other people's thoughts, all of the fearful watching, wondering and worrying. This is the ultimate lesson: How can you learn this now? It is the path to greater emotional freedom and ease, because there is only your process to figure out and work on, rather than trying to shape and manage other peoples' reliability and consistency.

Once you trust your ability to not only survive what comes your way, but to flourish and grow from it, all the energy that goes into doubt, fear and scrutinizing—all the time you spend worrying and obsessing—is suddenly released and you can use that energy to move toward what you love rather than away from what you fear.

What if we trusted ourselves and our ability to come out on the other side of any experience, trusted our incredible capacity to always find the light awaiting us on the other side of even the darkest moments? What if we truly knew in the deepest, most self-trusting way that no matter how dark life may be around us, that absolutely nothing can ever put out the light and love inside of us? Because that is what most questions of trust are about: Is it safe or smart to love this person or this experience? We often believe that if we send our love and light out to that which later hurts us, it will then damage the love inside of us.

The truth is, nothing can ever damage the love within us. Hurtful experiences may impact our courage, willingness, openness, or desire to trust and love again, but it is still within our power to always choose to express and extend love or to withhold and refuse to share it with others.

Learning to Trust

It is never wrong to love. It is always the right thing to offer out, although sometimes it is wise to refocus or rechannel your love from those who cannot reciprocate and channel it to those who know how to receive your love with gratitude and return it with enthusiasm. When you decide to trust yourself to love wisely and to learn new lessons when you realize that you aren't, there is so much less confusion, struggle and grief.

Suddenly there is nothing you need to do but trust, love and learn. You can trust yourself. All that you need is inside of you, including the ability to learn any new lesson. Unlearn your sense of impending danger. Trust that the best in you will prevail. Be your learner self. Be curious. Find out what happens when you look at trust differently. Trust that this learning, done in love and with love will bring you true freedom and safety. Trust is the ultimate triumph over fear and pain. Trust each moment for what it brings. Trust yourself.

Note to myself:

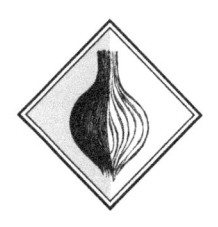

What behaviors, thoughts and feelings am I willing to peel away and let go of to be my most flourishing self?

CHAPTER 22

Finding Your Light

Where is your light? Where is the brightest part of your life force? Where are the most glorious, glimmering parts of your true self? Are you boldly shining in your daily life? Do you feel lost in trying to remember your light, in wondering what happened to it, when you saw it last and if you'll ever manage to see it again?

Society provides so many opportunities, so many invitations for us to get lost from our light. We get lost from our light by the demands and pressures of everyday life, from the false promises of things advertised to make us feel more alive but those things only serve to diminish our life force and dim our light. When our light dims not only do we lose, but those who interact with us lose as well. Whenever we fail to own, cherish and cultivate our light, we greatly reduce the scope of our own light as well as our ability to see others and ourselves accurately. The brighter our internal light, the greater our capacity to see beyond the limitations of ourselves and others, and the greater our ability to envision possibilities and potential waiting to unfold when we extend our effort, energy and light.

Peeling the Onion

There's a wonderful Viktor Frankl quote that I love: "That which brings light must endure burning." When I hear it I am reminded that cultivating and tending our light is not always easy and the commitment to choosing a life path that involves the conscious choice to always do whatever it takes to sustain and extend our light can often be filled with painful challenges and choices. Sometimes standing upright and strong in our light means standing still in the fire of other people's fear and blindness, in the fire of their reactivity and rage, and their power struggles and punishing behavior.

In order to endure the burning that can occur as you stand tall and clear in your light, you first must be really clear and ask yourself: What is my light? What about you is good and kind? Deeply aware and profound? Silly and sacred? Available and fully alive? What do you bring into the world everyday that makes the world a little brighter in quiet ways, in consistent ways, in wildly celebrating ways, in charming ways, in courageous ways?

What in you shows up and makes the world brighter, better, more anchored in what's good, in what's alive and passionate, in what's whimsical and wild? Where is your light? Where is your wild, bright hope? Where do you shine your light? What helps it glow? What causes it to flicker and falter? What do you need to do to retrieve any light that you've lost along the way?

And if you need to retrieve your light, then reclaiming your light means going back and remembering: What brought your light out as a child? What were the good things you noticed and cherished? Were those things in nature, in animals, in the elderly or in other simple pleasures? Was it touch or sensation, sound or sight, laughter or color, movement or books, or any other number of things?

Where did you see what was good as a teen? Where do you see what is good as an adult? Where do you wish you could see it now? What moments, even in the midst of challenges and obstacles, did you find the good? Where did you look? What pulled you through?

What do the kindest people in your life offer you? What are the places of light in yourself and other people that inspire you? What do you hunger to create more of in the world? What would you like to illuminate in yourself and bring more fully into the world?

If you had only one more year to live, what would you want to do with the light in you? My hope is that whatever your individual answer would be, that it would in part include a decision to shine your light as far and wide as possible, focusing on inviting others to join with their light. Can you imagine building on what's already good, right and strong, naming over and over how glorious it is, flourishing and feeling encouraged, hopeful, motivated, powerful, passionate, and fully alive?

There's no need to wait. Start right now. Turn on the lights, look inside, find everything that is lovely and good, bright and beautiful and let your amazing self come out of the shadows and shine. Be the light that refuses to flicker out. Be the light that does not leave. Be the light that has seen fear and sorrow and in seeing it, still chooses joy. Be the light in the winter storm. Be the light that helps others find their light and helps them shine.

Peeling the Onion

Note to myself:

What behaviors, thoughts and feelings am I willing to peel away and let go of to be my most flourishing self?

CHAPTER 21

Brilliance Everywhere

Have you ever noticed how dense people can seem sometimes, and just when you think someone's common sense couldn't get anymore microscopic it seems to absolutely disappear? Does it seem that as a culture we are cultivating the lowest common denominator in nearly everything? Do you ever wonder how we are going to turn it around?

Well, the solution is wonderfully simple: Start changing what you are looking for because if you are looking for examples of how people don't "Know their head from a hole in the ground" or "Wouldn't know a good deal if it jumped up and bit them" or dozens of other clichés that describe how inept and inadequate others are, that is exactly what you are going to find. Your days will be filled with seeing others in the most critical light and finding fault with them. If you look hard and long enough at anyone you can always find something they could have done better and it's a quick flip of the wrist to turn that into not being good enough and to turn not good enough into wrong and bad.

Peeling the Onion

So how do you change this? Start by looking for what others are doing that is brilliant and exactly right. Look for how others are learning, how they are making sense out of the lessons before them, growing, deepening their knowledge of themselves and what does and doesn't work for them.

Look for all the ways that what they are doing is smart, look for the flashes of brilliance in the way they approach their lives and name what you notice them doing right. Literally say, "That was a great way to handle that situation, how did you think to do it that way?" Let them explain their process to you and as they describe how they decided on their approach to the situation, they will start to internalize a vision of themselves as smart and capable. And guess what happens when people start to see themselves as smart? They start to behave in increasingly smart and capable ways.

The truth is that people are brilliant so much of the time. They are hilariously brilliant and creatively brilliant. They are brilliant with their surviving and with their flourishing, with their questioning and their questing for something more, with their hopes and with their courage.

People are brilliant grappling and wrestling with their stuck points and with their strategies for overcoming them. They are brilliant in their ways of seeking love and grieving loss. They are brilliant in pushing through hard times and in their capacity to celebrate good times. They are wise and wonderful, smart and good, full of brilliance in both the most mundane and miraculous of moments. There's so much of it all around, far more than our cynical society would ever dream was possible.

Begin now. Start looking at the people in the world around you. Practice saying "That was so smart" or "That's brilliant!" Point out

Brilliance Everywhere

someone's wisdom. Name exactly what someone did wisely or well. Look for it in kids, in teens, in adults, in groups, in strangers and in those closest to you. Look for it in yourself.

Watch for brilliance. Point it out. Make a big deal out of it. Dedicate yourself to being a professional, expert brilliance spotter. Do it all the time. Look for all the brilliance you can find. Help people see how amazing they are, inside and out.

Note to myself:

What behaviors, thoughts and feelings am I willing to peel away and let go of to be my most flourishing self?

CHAPTER 20

Carpet Angels

As a small child, one of my most favorite things in the world was to make snow angels. I loved everything about it—the falling backwards into fresh snow, the waving arms and legs to make the angel imprint and the heart-soaring joy I felt whenever I looked at a snowy field filled with a dozen snow angels pointing in every direction.

However, growing up in the Western Oregon often meant that we could go several years without seeing enough snow for the creation of snow angels. Given that this was one of the few true joys of my childhood, that often meant waiting through one winter and then another for the chance to do something that I loved. And my parents had neither the money nor the emotional responsiveness to ever think of transporting me to where we might find snow.

As children often do, I simply accepted these circumstances as fact, assumed they were unalterable and waited for the occasional moments where I could indulge my joy. Looking back now as an adult, I realize that my childhood experience of snow angels greatly reflected my parents' beliefs about joy. Joy hardly ever occurred and

Peeling the Onion

when it did, it was almost always unforeseen and therefore unpredictable in both its appearance and departure and it figuratively and literally was a random act of nature occurring absolutely outside of their control and consciousness.

It wasn't until the fall of my 24th year that I was able to see things differently. I was working as a graduate teaching fellow at the local university, leading discussion sessions for the film history professor. I had only been teaching for a few years at the time, and was still quite nervous when faculty would come into the class to observe me. Unfortunately that nervousness, coupled with naturally low blood pressure, caused me to get profoundly dizzy during one class session.

It was clear to me that I needed to lay down before I blacked out and fell down and even though I was being observed by faculty at the time, I really couldn't see any other options. I laid down, continued talking and as my students laughed and the faculty members stared and I started moving my arms and legs back and forth because my hands and feet were tingling. I started laughing, recognizing the movements from an earlier time and said, "You know, I laid down because I got dizzy, but now that I'm down here, I realized you can make great carpet angels by waving your arms and legs around." I encouraged my students to try it and soon the class was on the floor, all making carpet angels with me.

I managed in some vague, tangential way to link the carpet angels into some thematic element of whatever film we were discussing and the feedback later from the faculty was that what I had done was wonderfully creative, interactive and a big success. Much more important to me, however, was the enormous light bulb that clicked on the moment I was making carpet angels.

Carpet Angels

The light bulb was this: Stop waiting for the ideal external circumstances for joy and just embrace any circumstance and create the joy now. Not tomorrow, not next year if it snows, but right here, right now. The joy I got from making carpet angels was no less than the joy I got from making snow angels, and when I realized I could make angel imprints wherever and whenever I wanted, I began to do it all over the place.

I made meadow angels and beach angels, pine needle angels and autumn leaf angels. I made angels in airports when planes were delayed, angels at graduations and housewarmings, angels in hospital rooms, at picnics and camping sites. Anytime the mood hit me, I threw myself down and made angel imprints and invited the people around me to join in. I laughed and told them how good it feels to leave the imprint of an angel behind in a world that can use all of the angel energy and joy that can be mustered.

Move toward what you love and what brings you joy. Stop waiting for it to be the right time or the right conditions. Dive into what you love. Look for every chance to romp with what delights you. Swing dance with your soul. Belt out made-up songs. Remember what makes you giggle. Look for passion and playfulness and embrace it when you see it. Create joy without waiting for snow.

Peeling the Onion

Note to myself:

What behaviors, thoughts and feelings am I willing to peel away and let go of to be my most flourishing self?

Chapter 19

Small Ears of Corn

How often in our closest relationships do we feel a mixture of frustration and despair over the things we perceive that are not readily forthcoming from the other person? And how often do we succumb to the tidal tug of our Western culture by insisting, cajoling, whining, shouting, pouting, manipulating or pressuring the other person to change and be more of whatever we believe is missing in our relationship? Does this ever work, truly work, other than in the most temporary, begrudgingly minimal ways? We know the answer. People don't change in lasting, ongoing ways unless they choose to grow.

It is such a hard concept for many people to grasp emotionally: No one changes unless they want to change. I am amazed at the number of clients and students I see who struggle in seemingly endless ways to try to make that statement not be true in their relationships. I watch them put enormous amounts of painful, unrewarding and exhausting effort into anything other than simply accepting who the person is rather than who they want the person to be.

Peeling the Onion

I absolutely believe it is essential to give our partners clear information on how we wish to be treated, behaviors that we especially value and appreciate and the ways in which we feel most cared for and loved. I also believe that once that has been communicated clearly and the other person is not acting on that information, it is because the person isn't interested enough or fully able to enact that change. Tempting as it might be to delve into why the change is not occurring, the search for the "whys" only postpones the one essential task before you: To accept that the other person is not going to show up with what you want.

Did you notice that I said accept, not like, or agree or be happy with the fact? It can feel very difficult to accept the truth of what the person in your life is and isn't offering you, and to make some clear decisions regarding what that means to you. So many women expend an enormous amount of energy feeling angry and hurt that their loved one isn't giving them what they want (which unfortunately never gets them more of what they want), instead of using that same energy to decide what to do next regarding their situation.

The image that often helps me remain clear-headed in these circumstances is to think about cornstalks and ears of corn. I envision the person that I am wanting more from as a large corn stalk and whatever I want more of as a small ear of corn on the stalk. So what if I would like more affection from Ted—let's say ears of corn the size of a Buick and right now his level of affection is much smaller, like the size of bug mittens? Rather than be hurt, disappointed or angry at Ted, I can just accept that while one day it might change, right now he has extremely small ears of corn that aren't fully grown.

Small Ears of Corn

For me this metaphor serves several purposes. It helps me remember that a person's level of growth is whatever it is and that persuading and arguing doesn't make the corn grow any faster. Also, growth has to come from within, be it corn or human growth. In addition, just as it would make no sense to stand in front of a corn stalk and say, "If you loved me your ears of corn would be bigger," it also makes no sense to say "If you loved me, you'd show me more affection," because the person is exactly where they are regardless of what you'd prefer.

The other helpful thing this metaphor assists me in remembering is that I have a choice. I can look at the person I love and factually acknowledge to myself that they have small ears of corn in an area that I wish they had larger ears and then I can be aware that I have several options available to me. I can choose to wait and see if any growth occurs. I can seek to have that preference met in other appropriate ways with other individuals while remaining in the relationship. I can decide to leave the relationship or I can decide that receiving affection isn't that central to my well being after all. What I decide isn't nearly as important as the act of deciding itself. Within the decision is the acceptance that I'm dealing with small ears of corn that may or may not get bigger and that it would be ridiculous to be furious at the corn for its size or to organize my life around being happy when the corn is finally big enough.

When what I want isn't happening in a relationship, I shrug my shoulders and say to myself, "Small ears of corn." This helps me remember that the corn isn't wrong for being the size it is and I'm not wrong for wanting larger ears of corn. When I let go of being mad or sad about what isn't there I can make a calm choice about whether to stay or go, wait for what I'd like, seek it out elsewhere

Peeling the Onion

or shift my preferences. Regardless of the option chosen, it gets me out of the corn field, keeps me from shouting "Grow, damn it!" and allows me to put my energy into more rewarding and powerful ways to live my life.

Most of the time people's lack of immediate growth isn't because they don't love or value us enough. It's simply that they grow at their own speed, which is comprised of their own unique blend of fear and desire, belief and doubt, daring and dread. Everything grows, if it's meant to, in it's own way and time. There's no point in feeling angry because it has nothing to do with you, good or bad. Anytime you find yourself insisting that someone should be different, just remember these four words: Small ears of corn.

Note to myself:

What behaviors, thoughts and feelings am I willing to peel away and let go of to be my most flourishing self?

CHAPTER 18

Sitting in Mud Puddles

This is a story about my childhood. It isn't a happy story, so if those things trouble you, you might want to pass this chapter by and wait for the happier chapters that follow.

All of the sides of family life that the Brady Bunch and other cheerful family shows failed to present—violence, sexual and emotional abuse, drug and alcohol addiction, mental illness and poverty—all of those things were alive and deeply unwell in my family. My earliest, clearest memories are of sitting cross-legged on the scratch gray fabric of what was then called a davenport, tugging on the edges of my elastic depleted, dirty, mismatched socks as I tried to decipher how to keep my three-and-a half year old self safe from the raging chaos, untreated mental illness and explosive violence that made up my daily life.

Obviously, at that age I had no language or understanding of what was truly going on. All I knew was that sometimes my mother left me alone and nothing bad happened, and sometimes she was terrifyingly angry, shouting and crying for hours about things that made no sense to me. Sometimes these episodes would end with

Peeling the Onion

her laying her exhausted self down on the davenport, putting her still-crying head on my lap, while I petted her head until she fell into a restless sleep. Other times the episodes would end with her directly screaming at me, lunging at me and slapping me repeatedly, trying to make me cry.

Being stubborn, I refused to cry and would look straight into her eyes and hold my gaze steady as I looked at her. This infuriated her even more, seeing my large golden eyes that held no harm or hatred simply looking back at her. She would then yank me up roughly and carry me outside to the long, rutted gravel driveway that connected our house to the main highway. In freezing, wet Oregon weather she would then drop me into a large mud puddle and order me to not move until she told me to move. She would leave me there for what seemed like hours and my legs would grow icy and numb as I sat there in my too-small cotton dress and mismatched socks.

Over time I began to watch for the subtle and not so subtle shifts in her energy and voice that preceded the long hours of screaming and crying. Even though there was no way that I could ascertain whether her raging would end in her falling asleep or slamming me down in a freezing mud puddle, I began to dread the not knowing even more than the possible outcome. And so, at age four, at the point where her screaming and slamming of objects had rapidly escalated in volume and intensity, I would walk over to the front door, open it and walk over to the driveway and sit down in the first muddle puddle I came upon.

Even though not every episode with my mother ended with her hitting me and dropping me in the water, I just couldn't stand the possibility of waiting to see if harm was going to come my way yet again. Better to know it, be in charge of it, do it and get it over with. Better to voluntarily freeze my child spirit than to let her repeatedly try to drown it.

For the next two years until I went to first grade, I dodged her rage as best I could, being silent and invisible whenever possible, sitting myself in mud puddles when it was not. My child spirit flickered but refused to go out, dreaming of the day I could climb on the long yellow school bus and never be left alone with her again.

School came and rescued me, gave me safe dry rooms bright with books and teachers' faces, gave me structure and support, a place where the rules made sense and stayed the same, where I was treated warmly, gently and well. School and wonderfully loving and perceptive teachers sustained me until I was able to leave home for good.

It was only then as an adult, finally safe from the chaos and danger of my childhood, that I realized how truly fearful I was that something bad was continually on the verge of happening out of nowhere. This fear that I had carried forward from my childhood also came with my absolute dread of the unknown and my insistence that I was going to be in charge of whatever pain I experienced. This was a brilliant childhood coping mechanism, yet deeply unproductive and unsatisfying as an adult.

I watched myself as I did the adult equivalent of throwing myself down in mud puddles. I left relationships before I could be left, got tired of jobs before they grew tired of me, changed majors before someone could decide I had no talent, gained weight before someone could decided they were attracted to someone else, and the list of other mud puddle moments went on and on.

Peeling the Onion

I radically disrupted any opportunities for anything truly good to come my way because I couldn't stand the tension of wondering when the next awful, out-of-control thing was going to happen. It was incredibly difficult to break this habit. Many times I would catch myself only after I had again succumbed to the gravitational pull of the mud puddle and I would then pull myself out of my self-created pain and start to explore what was behind my fear.

Invariably, it almost always had to do with something positive abruptly ending, without warning and absolutely out of my control to impact the outcome. My dread of this was nearly unbearable and I would watch myself, over and over again, wade into self-created pain all in an attempt to avoid facing my early childhood powerlessness in the midst of seemingly endless violence and pain.

What finally allowed me to let go of my old behaviors and just let life unfold was a two-fold piece of awareness. First, although pain does sometimes show up out of the blue with absolutely no warning, so does joy, yet my strategy only guaranteed pain because I assumed the pain was inevitable and therefore created it rather than pausing and waiting for the joy that was possible to emerge and surprise me.

The second piece of awareness was that that everything ends, incredibly great things and incredibly horrid things, all of it at some point ends. Being afraid of endings suddenly started feeling like being afraid of rain. I could live my life in fear of losing everything, in fear of the good weather going away. I could spend my life standing in the sprinkler spray so I could pretend I actually chose the rain when it came or I could accept that while the rain does sometimes come, it also goes and good weather always eventually follows.

Sitting in Mud Puddles

So, as I gave up the illusion of trying to have control over the uncontrollable, I gained joy and peace in embracing reality as it unfolded in my life. How do you face this? Are there circumstances in life, kinds of uncertainty, moments or events in which the outcome is unknown where you move yourself to your own emotional or behavioral mud puddles?

Where do you automatically plunk yourself down in pain rather than pausing to see if joy is possible? What happy outcome do you assume is not possible and how do you derail yourself into your own mud puddles? What if you asked yourself, "What else besides pain is possible?" Let life show you all the other positive ways things can unfold. What if you looked for the happy ending and trusted yourself and life enough to start moving toward it?

You've had plenty of the pain. Don't you think some of the pleasure, beauty and kindness in the world belong to you too? It's time to climb out of the mud puddles.

Note to myself:

What behaviors, thoughts and feelings am I willing to peel away and let go of to be my most flourishing self?

CHAPTER 17

I Think I Can, I Think I Can, I Think I Can Stop Trying

One of my favorite books when I was seven or eight was The Little Engine That Could. I loved the book and deeply internalized the message of trying, trying, trying and started throwing myself into any situation where I could prove that I could make good outcomes happen. The more impossible the task, the more powerful the expenditure of life force, the greater the intensity of the quest, the more I was committed to trying. Unfortunately, this act of trying was often focused on trying to win the unwinnable.

Fast forward to adulthood, where my early childhood devotion to trying had been joined with an unfortunately high tolerance for unacceptable behavior and an increasingly shaky sense of self-esteem. All of this perfectly prepared me for my early adult quest as a woman: To try and try and try to prove that I was lovable and worthy of not being abandoned or otherwise tossed aside for someone else.

And, oh how I tried. Like anything else I do, good or bad, I did it big, embarrassingly big. I turned myself into whatever the person in front of me wanted and, therefore I presumed found lovable.

Peeling the Onion

You want goddess? I was serene, sublime and transcendent. You want wild? I was daring, irreverent and fearless. You want intellectual? I was bright, articulate, well read and deeply analytical. You want charismatic? I was witty, charming and totally engaging. You want athletic? I was energetic, sweaty, competitive and strong.

You get the picture, there was no true picture of me because I was always changing my presentation of myself to try to win the person's attention, affection, admiration and respect—to prove that I had what it took to be truly loved by someone. The problem was I was never being myself. I was always obsessed with trying to win acceptance and therefore I had never devoted any time to figuring out who I truly was, but the one thing I knew was that I wasn't being authentic because I was constantly changing who I was based on whose affection I was trying to win.

In addition, I distanced myself even more from any discovery of what my true self actually was by investing whatever energy I had left into strategizing new and more effective ways to be able to try even harder. I spent hours talking with friends and analyzing how I could demonstrate in progressively more amazing ways why it made such good sense to decide to love me.

The horrible truth of all of this is that none of it worked. All of my colossal energy and all of the Olympic level intensity that I threw into my trying never changed a thing. The people who didn't want to love me didn't love me. The people who wanted to leave me left. The people who didn't want to give me the things I wanted never changed their minds and did anything differently. I could have never once indulged in trying behavior and simply been my day-to-day, kind, warm and intelligent self, saved the energy and the outcome would have been the same. So why did I do this, and

I Think I Can, I Think I Can, I Think I Can Stop Trying

why do all of you who are nodding your heads in recognition as you read this, why do we do something so painful, exhausting and profoundly unproductive?

Well, here's my theory about where the seeds of this behavior come from: Children are far more perceptive than we realize and most children are very capable of accurately gauging if the important adults in their lives are able to be present and fully love them and this is where the difficulty lies. What do young children do when they realize, on whatever level, that the adults around them are not capable of providing a consistent, profound and loving relationship? For most children, actually allowing this awareness into the clear, conscious light of day would be far too hopeless and devastating. How would a five year old with no car keys and no wallet, and therefore no way out, face the prospect of living without real love for 13 more years, especially when at that age a week feels like an eternity?

Instead of acknowledging that there is no opportunity to form a consistent, profound, loving relationship with the adults in their immediate environment, children do the next best thing: They throw all their energy into forming a consistent, profound, loving relationship by trying to create lovable selves. They commit to it, invest in it, all with the hope that if they stay fully engaged in trying to become lovable, they will find the magic combination of behaviors that with cause the adults around them to suddenly become capable of loving them.

Tragic as it sounds, virtually every child would rather feel it is her that is unlovable and that explains the lack of love, rather than absorb the harsh truth that the adults in their midst do not know how to love her warmly, wisely or well. If a child can believe it's

Peeling the Onion

something about her, well then she has a project, some direction to take, some impact and power over the situation. If the love isn't there yet, it's just because she hasn't tried hard enough yet, but with more trying she still has the chance to be victorious. On the surface that has so much more power than absorbing the actual truth that some people are so damaged or emotionally dead inside that they will never be capable of loving others well.

Why is it that we are willing to accept that some people will most likely never be capable of walking or seeing, yet we resist identifying people as unable to love? Wouldn't life be much easier if everyone who was unable to love just drove around with a bumper sticker stuck to the car that had a heart in a circle with a slash through it? Wouldn't that be freeing? You would just shrug your shoulders and say, "Well, no point in even trying." Which brings me full circle to my original point. As much as I wish it were otherwise, the act of over-trying never changes the truth: The people who will really, truly, wonderfully love you will do so without you ever having to try, try, try to get them to love you.

It's here that the growing pains kick in—because as unfulfilling as a relationship with trying and striving can be, you are actually the only one in the relationship. You are totally in charge of it, even when it doesn't go well. If you actually let go of your relationship with trying and begin having a relationship with someone who loves you as you are, you've gained a lot of authentic love but lost the sense of having all of the power because you're sharing it with the other person. Sometimes I think that's why people have such a hard time believing they are enough—not because they don't believe they are, but because if they believe it then they'll have to stop having a relationship with over-trying and actually have

I Think I Can, I Think I Can, I Think I Can Stop Trying

a relationship with a real person and open up to feeling loved, vulnerable and connected.

I'll always be a big fan of striving, growing and evolving. I think it's great when people learn new skills, deepen their self-knowledge, explore creativity or get curious about what else is possible for them. What makes these behaviors something lovely and self-honoring rather than laborious and self-diminishing is the intention that the person brings to those pursuits. Do what you do out of delight and desire that resonates in you rather than attempting to demonstrate your worth. Stop trying to be loved and just go live life in the ways that fit you best. Let love, real love that you never have work to for or worry about, find you there.

Note to myself:

What behaviors, thoughts and feelings am I willing to peel away and let go of to be my most flourishing self?

CHAPTER 16

Infant Time

Somewhere, in all the endless stacks of reading that I was both required and inspired to do in the process of earning my Ph.D. in psychology, I came across the concept of infant time. Suffice it to say that it struck me as an incredibly useful way to reframe experiences that many of us find both common and distressing. The premise behind this concept is that under normal, relatively crisis-free adult life, most of us manage to maintain a fairly realistic conceptualization of the duration of experiences as they relate to the passage of time.

We are able to grasp and retain that our visit to the dentist will consist of being in the dentist chair for 60 minutes and at the end of that time, we will leave there and proceed into the next part of our day. This adult understanding and conceptualization of time allows us to engage in numerous life events, both enjoyable and mundane, and understand that most everything has a beginning, middle and end to it. Because of this knowledge, we are usually able to convince ourselves to do things that may not be our first choice of activities because we are able to understand that we will not *always* be engaged in that activity.

Peeling the Onion

For some reason, the capacity to view life experiences in this way begins to shift and sometimes unravel when we are faced with events that we find challenging or frightening. Many of us, when faced with this dilemma, lose our sturdy adult perspective of time and shift into the realm of infant time.

So what exactly is infant time? Imagine for a moment, life from the perspective of an infant who is only aware of the experience that is happening right now. She has no memory of what her experience was ten minutes ago and no cognitive capacity to conceive of a future ten minutes from now because the future simply doesn't exist for her.

In this realm of infant time, whatever is being experienced in the moment is the only thing that is real, no other experience has ever existed and no other possibilities exist on the horizon because there is no horizon. In infant time, whatever is true in the moment is all that will ever be known, so the moment *is* eternity.

Think about this for a moment. Let's say this infant girl had a dry diaper just five minutes ago, but now it's wet, and she begins to cry with mounting intensity. It is her experience that the wetness is intolerable in part because she has no recollection of the earlier experience of being dry. For her, she is wet now and she'll be wet forever.

Well, it seems as though a similar experience gets mobilized when adults face challenging circumstances and they revert to infant time. Whatever is occurring in the moment—a health crisis, grieving over the loss of person, relationship or way of life—feels that it will seemingly go on forever. This has a great deal to do with why you hear people say things like "I know I'll never feel the same again," or "No matter what anyone says, I

Infant Time

know I'll always be alone," or "I don't think this feeling will ever go away."

And it seems that no matter how much you remind them that other bad and hurtful experiences have passed, they perceive this current situation as different and therefore never ending. This can be a very helpful notion to remember when you're facing difficulties: Expect your conception of time to revert to infant time. Watch for your use of the words always and never, especially in relation to your feelings. The truth is everything ends, terrific feelings as well as painful feelings. It's just that no one ever says, "Oh, thank goodness all that warm contentment is finally gone." We are usually worried the good feelings won't last long enough and that the bad feelings will last far too long.

One helpful thought to hang on to if you feel yourself sliding into infant time is something that I was told when I was being trained to work on a crisis line. My instructor stated that a true crisis cannot last longer than six weeks, and after six weeks the panicky crisis feeling is gone and it moves into a more settled stressful situation or the crisis gets resolved. Whether or not this is even remotely accurate, I love the idea of this because as yucky as a crisis can be, I always feel I can survive anything for six weeks as much as I may dislike the experience. I just tell myself that I have perhaps another five and a half weeks of feeling this intensely and then I'll be in a bit of a different place.

Another thing that helps me, especially when facing major challenges (like grieving the death of loved ones), is to remind myself that no matter how intense the sorrow or despair that my current emotional state is only a snapshot of the moment. This snapshot of the moment is capturing this moment in time and that

Peeling the Onion

might feel radically different two hours from now when I am in dance class lost in the bliss of the music and the movement.

No matter how bad the situation is, it is only bad for now. Life never becomes frozen. The bad moment *will* go away and be replaced with something beautiful. Those who have stopped loving or living will be followed by others who are still loving and living. Lost ways of life will be followed by newly discovered ways of being. Everything eventually changes and this will too. Time is always on your side because time always brings new things and some of those things statistically have to be good because it's statistically impossible that it won't happen. You can stay out of infant time. Better moments are on their way.

Note to myself:

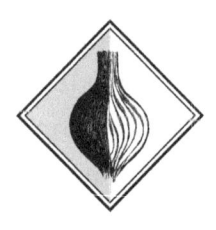

What behaviors, thoughts and feelings am I willing to peel away and let go of to be my most flourishing self?

CHAPTER 15

Pineapple Upside Down Cake

Have you ever made pineapple upside down cake? The very first thing to go into the bottom of the pan is this wonderful mixture of brown sugar, butter and pineapple rings. Once this magnificent, sugary layer is in place, then cupfuls of golden cake batter are added to fill the cake pan. The cake is then baked and once it is cooled, the pan is flipped over and the cake comes out with the ingredients that went in first now on the top of the cake.

As a child, I loved the idea that something that starts at the bottom in the beginning ends up on the top at the end. Even though I never cared much for the cake itself as a desert, I still think that the concept of it is very cool, both as an interesting way to construct a cake and as a helpful metaphor to look at early developmental emotional needs.

Let me explain what I mean. Have you ever found yourself feeling stuck, feeling as though you're missing some vital piece of early nurturing that's left you with this hole inside, that no matter what you do or what others offer you that nothing quite manages to take away that hollow feeling? Even when others are well inten-

Peeling the Onion

tioned and try to offer you what they think will help, do you find that it doesn't fit with what you need to feel better?

Well, there are good reasons for those feelings. Often the feeling of being empty or hollow comes from our earliest experiences of having primary core needs deeply unmet. These unmet needs can occur in incredibly healthy families all the way to horrifically unhealthy families. Most of us are familiar with the list of elements detrimental to good nurturing experiences: Addiction, abuse, violence, mental illness and so on. Yet even in the most loving family a child's core needs might be poorly met due to variables outside the control of even the most nurturing parents. Sometimes physical illness interferes with consistent care during a vital developmental stage, sometimes radical differences in temperament and energy can make it difficult for a differently-styled parent to generate developmental experiences for a child. Two very introverted parents raising a highly extroverted child whose needs for celebration of her larger-than-life curiosity and expansiveness may find that they cannot, despite their best intentions, meet their child's need to have her parents mirror back enthusiasm for her outgoing personality.

So what do you do if you feel as though you have missed out on early, vital, affirming, nurturing experiences and you don't want to continue to walk around with a big gaping hole inside of you? This is what I suggest: Start viewing your experiences as a pineapple upside down cake. Know that the things you most often feel that you are missing are the elements that go in first—the brown sugar, pineapple and butter. These powerful flavors are supposed to come in your early childhood experiences and the

Pineapple Upside Down Cake

cake batter comes as you grow, through school and career, through teen and adult experiences.

One of the major difficulties is that if you missed the great gooey layers of things, no matter how many generous cups of cake batter loving friends, partners and coworkers may offer you, it's not the amazing sweet layer that you missed in your early years and you may feel the kid voice in you say, "But that's not what I waaaaaaaant!" The truth is, nothing will take the place of what you missed early on, but that doesn't mean that you push away the amazing gifts that the people in your life can offer you.

One of the biggest mistakes people make is insisting that others put pineapple rings into their cake pans, and feeling upset when they are offered a cup of cake batter. Guess what? No one was responsible for putting down that early layer but your caretakers and if that didn't happen it is horribly unfair to ask another adult to take care of it now. It's not their job and they didn't sign on for it. Besides, it never works.

If you missed out on vital experiences or basic nurturing you have two main choices. Figure out a way to give yourself those experiences or if this doesn't work, then find a therapist to help you fill the hollow places with the experiences that you need. It's okay to assert your desire to get that lovely first layer down, just don't turn up your nose at all the amazing cups of batter that loving individuals are willing to offer you right this minute.

Peeling the Onion

Note to myself:

What behaviors, thoughts and feelings am I willing to peel away and let go of to be my most flourishing self?

Chapter 14

Don't Organize Around Chaos

Sometimes the people we love the most, while being infinitely valuable and lovable, are also immensely immersed in a chaotic lifestyle. One of the largest challenges you face is that precisely because you *do* love this person and you want to have them in your life, their chaos can start to feel like it is becoming your chaos because chaos can be highly contagious.

The tough thing about chaos is that, well, it's chaotic. This means it is generally unpredictable (although some people's style of chaos can get predictable over the years), and when it kicks in, whatever passes for normal life gets disrupted or absolutely derailed. Why is it that when the chaos passes, the person who tends to engage in chaos as a way of life tends to feel rejuvenated and refreshed while the rest of us are absolutely wiped out and gasping for breath?

It is absolutely essential that you stop organizing around chaos. If you continue to arrange your life around managing, minimizing or containing the damage done by someone with a chaotic lifestyle you will ultimately spend the very best of your creative life force trying to achieve the unachievable: To create order and peace for

Peeling the Onion

someone who is in a cycle of stress, panic, poor impulse control and bad decision making.

Chaotic lifestyles are usually present in people with unresolved pain. The major purpose of the chaos is to create external pain that can be identified, grappled with, and dramatically dealt with, often with the help of others. The difficulty with this strategy is that although it protects the person by keeping them busy dealing with the external chaos, the person never deals with the internal emotional pain and never gets a chance to resolve it. Failing to deal with the internal emotional pain comes at a high price and that high price is having a life that does not work well, a life that jarringly ricochets between blow up and clean up.

Lost are the lovely moments, the peaceful luxury of uneventful days where there is time to focus on growth, on making positive changes, on moving through the past and going forward. Lost also is the safety that comes when the people you love are actively addressing any unresolved internal pain rather than creating externalized pain that you have to deal with and try to contain. Their self-generated chaos creates behavioral symptoms and diseases: Drug and alcohol abuse and addiction, eating disorders, sexual and gambling addictions, infidelity, violence and abuse of any kind.

Your first step in not organizing around chaos is to refuse to have a relationship with the chaos. Your relationship is with the person not their chaos. In order to be able to truly do this, you need to know that you can leave this person if, only temporarily, because if you are economically or emotionally dependent on them you will be held hostage by their chaos. You will feel that you need to manage their chaos rather than manage your own life. Trust me, as scary as it may be to claim your full independence and manage

Don't Organize Around Chaos

your own life, it is always much easier to do that than to attempt to manage another person's life.

It is absolutely essential that you learn to organize around your own continuity, your own rhythms, maintaining the life focus that keeps your life on track and moving forward. It means that you do not get hooked into the role of rescuer or resource provider. Your only responsibility is to have appropriate empathy for the dilemma the person is in and name any useful resources you think might be helpful. Remain aware that the true source of the despair, panic and fear that you see before you has nothing to do with external events of your mother's bulimia and resulting dental problems, or your boyfriend's addiction and resulting unemployment. Certainly those events cause pain, but they are not the cause of the pain.

You didn't cause the unhealed pain, you didn't break what is broken and you can't fix it regardless of how patient and brilliant you are and how much you want to help. Your job is to stay on the path of living a healthy life and finding and sustaining whatever allows you to have a productive mix of balance and growth.

Anytime you get tempted to organize around chaos, picture the chaos as garbage can lids blowing around in a windstorm. Would you really race around trying to catch the lids or would you go inside so you could prevent your head from getting sliced off by something out of your control? Hold your position. Find your center. Stand solid and let the chaos blow past you. Don't chase garbage can lids.

Peeling the Onion

Note to myself:

What behaviors, thoughts and feelings am I willing to peel away and let go of to be my most flourishing self?

CHAPTER 13

Cherish Yourself

Nearly all of us long to be deeply cherished by those that we value. I have spent an enormous amount of my life force longing to be cherished by the people that I deemed most important, starting with my father and moving through other men who were in effect merely stand-ins for him.

The truth is that my father was fundamentally incapable of cherishing *anything* because he could not value anything except for its use to him in the most practical of terms or as a balm to the tremendous black hole of pain that he was alternately oblivious to or otherwise unwilling to address. Unfortunately, as is often the case with children, his pain became mine and his fundamental inability to cherish anything became my experience of feeling deeply and profoundly under-cherished.

I took this feeling forward through life and struggled against the illogic of this presumption: How could I not be worth cherishing when a wonderful array of loving friends, appreciative students and grateful clients found me loving and easy to cherish? Yet I continued to bang my head against romantic experiences in which

Peeling the Onion

the end equation was always the same: I didn't count for much and I was entirely replaceable and rarely cherished.

Never mind that literally every one of those men (I kid you not) eventually circled back around and told me how they blew it and how they had never gotten over me. Still, the damage was done because I had been discarded and deeply under-cherished.

So what was the way out of this sickening, horribly repetitive, painful pattern? Simply this: I finally stopped trying to prove why someone should want to cherish me, why I was worthwhile and why I shouldn't be discarded this week.

Trying to prove my worth was painful, an enormous amount of work, ineffective and ultimately pointless. It was like trying to convince someone of gravity. I knew it was there but how do you prove something to someone who can't see it? And more importantly, why bother? We merit cherishing regardless of the depth and breadth of anyone's denseness, addiction, abuse, mental illness, misuse of power or core level cruelty. We are beautiful, kind, wise, loving and infinitely worthy of genuinely loving and cherishing behavior.

It's absolutely all right if someone isn't at the stage where they can recognize, celebrate and cherish you. Instead of trying to convince or educate them, just smile warmly, step aside and clear the way for someone with the wisdom to realize that they have hit the jackpot to have you in their life. Cherish yourself and cherishing others will come.

Cherish Yourself

Note to myself:

What behaviors, thoughts and feelings am I willing to peel away and let go of to be my most flourishing self?

CHAPTER 12

Don't Listen to the Birds in Your Head

One of my earliest experiences as a new counselor was doing intake assessments on prospective clients who were seeking services at our low cost university counseling clinic. Since our clinic was a training facility for Master's and Ph.D. therapists, one of the goals of the new client assessment was to identify any individuals who might have mental health issues that would be too challenging given the experience level of the therapists working there.

Those of us conducting the assessments were given a list of questions to ask each potential new client. One question stirred up my new therapist nervousness: "Do you ever hear or see things that others can't see or hear or that might not really be there?" When I asked my supervisor what I was supposed to do if someone answered yes, she told me not to worry because that virtually never happened. Well, she was right. I asked that question in dozens and dozens of new client interviews and everyone said no, until one rainy February afternoon.

A thirty-year old woman came in complaining of low energy and dissatisfaction with her current job. She stated that she wanted

Peeling the Onion

to see a therapist to explore her low energy and what other career directions might be appropriate for her. All of this seemed absolutely straightforward as she and I proceeded with the intake process.

The rest of her responses seemed equally straightforward and as we neared the end of the intake, I asked her the question about if she was hearing and seeing things that aren't there, and I was expecting to get the customary "no" response. While the first word out of her mouth was "no," it was quickly followed by, "Except for those two big black birds sitting up in the corner of the room above your head." So what did I do? I turned around to look up at the spot she had just pointed to, which was a definite sign that I was a new therapist.

Seeing nothing there and trying to regain whatever scraps of professional composure that I still had, I turned back to her and asked, "And what are they saying?" She answered, "They usually tell me to hurt people, but they like you." Whew! Good for me, I thought and with that positive endorsement I finished the assessment and referred her to an appropriate agency in the community.

As the years passed, I found my thoughts returning to that woman and the image of those two birds following her throughout her life, telling her that everyone was dangerous and that it was important to hurt others before they hurt her. What a rough, scary way to go through life, and yet how many of us carry a symbolic version of those birds around with us? How many of us have an internal voice that says unhelpful, frightening things like "You're not good enough," or "No one will ever love you," or "You'll never be a success at anything" or any other number of painful things that aren't remotely true but still feel true? And just because you don't actually see the birds move their beaks when you hear those horrible words it still doesn't make the words feel any less devastating or inescapable.

Couple that with the notion that most of us are contending with our symbolic, invisible bird voices and very likely occupied with trying to keep them at bay, it's a wonder that we have the energy or ability to attempt to accurately listen to what another person is trying to communicate. Visualize two people trying to have a conversation. While the actual conversation is occurring there is a second conversation going on in bird world: "I don't think she likes me" or "She's looking at me like I am stupid." It's no wonder that communication can feel complicated and that people can behave in ways that don't make sense when we realize that there can be multiple layers of conversation happening simultaneously.

So what do you do if this is occurring for you? First, get clear on the differences between your terrorizing "bird chatter" and your gut instincts or intuition that provides you with good input beyond what can be concretely seen or measured. This form of knowing is invaluable and can provide you with vital information to keep you safe and help you make wise decisions. This form of knowing most often surfaces in quiet, peaceful ways when there is time and space for the knowledge and information to emerge.

Terrorizing bird chatter is just the opposite: It consists of anxious, jangling, loud, relentless and aggressive thoughts that keep you scared, insecure, afraid to trust yourself, to trust others and to take healthy risks in your life. The bird chatter is the voice of fear rather than the wise voice of caution. The chatter makes you more afraid, less creative and flexible in your responses, tries to

Peeling the Onion

get you to react in the same patterns that have always brought you pain, limitations and heartache.

The bird chatter doesn't help you. It's not here to protect you. It's not your friend. It doesn't believe anything good is possible for you. Here's what I want you to hear: It's absolutely dead wrong. Period. It's time to stop listening to the birds in your head and time to listen to your intuition and to your heart. Start believing that good things are possible. Start truly believing that good things are possible for you.

Note to myself:

What behaviors, thoughts and feelings am I willing to peel away and let go of to be my most flourishing self?

CHAPTER 11

Create the Energy that is Missing

What is the emotional energy that you're currently missing the most in your daily life? What do you crave that no matter what you do or how hard you try that you still feel you can't access enough of to fully satisfy yourself? Is it love, appreciation, attention, enthusiasm, consideration or respect?

Whatever your answers are to the above questions, one thing is clear: You are not having the emotional experiences that you most desire. More importantly, what do you do when you realize this is the case? Do you try to bargain, wheedle, pout, motivate or bully that emotion out of others? Do you just resign yourself to not having it and feel helpless and hopeless about ever getting what you want?

How about a third option? What if you took charge of creating the very energy that you feel is missing in your life? What if you said, "I'm tired of not having passionate, all-encompassing love in my life and I intend on doing something about it right now?" What if instead of wishing, waiting and wondering if the love you

Peeling the Onion

desire will ever find you, that you instead turned your energies toward creating what seems to allude you?

So how would you do that if what you long for is to experience passionate, all-encompassing love? First of all, you will need to let go of the insistence that you have to be the recipient of that energy in order to experience the feeling of it. While that might indeed be your preference, if your true goal is to feel passionate, all-encompassing love in your life then you need to take steps to be in charge of the production of that emotion, not just sitting on the loading dock waiting for a delivery of something that may never arrive.

What does "be in charge of that feeling" mean? It means that if you want to feel love in your life, you begin by responding to the world with love. Your task is to embody the loving energy you desire in the way you view others, their strengths and struggles, their interactions and avoidances—that you express an attitude of love and active interest in the person in front of you. It means that you stop waiting to be in love with a person and that you start being in love with the world and within reason most everything in it. You stop waiting for that emotional experience to come to you and instead you go into the world and act as if the experience is already true and ongoing.

Every day you get up and make a fresh choice, a fresh commitment to be the core elements of the energy you most long to experience. You go into the world with the experience of love already alive inside of you and live from that place, expressing it every chance you get. And in the expressing of it and people's response to it, irony of all ironies, you will find yourself surrounded by the very experience of the energy you longed for—people will

Create the Energy that is Missing

be sharing their appreciation of the loving energy that you have produced and extended to them.

Wake up tomorrow and make a conscious decision to offer out what you feel is most missing from your life—peace, hope, humor, or happiness. Take every opportunity to create it regardless of how brief the moment or how transitory the interaction. Notice how many hundreds of chances you have every day to generate the energy that is missing. Chances are that if you are missing it that others are as well.

If you are hungry for apples, you can sit, wait and hope someone brings you apples. Or you can go shopping for apples and see if you can buy or bargain for them. Or you can follow Johnny Appleseed's lead and plant apple trees so that there are apples enough for you and anyone else who is hungry for apples. It is that way with love too. Be a Johnny Appleseed and let love grow around you wherever you go.

Note to myself:

What behaviors, thoughts and feelings am I willing to peel away and let go of to be my most flourishing self?

CHAPTER 10

Name it, Blame it, and Claim it

Whining gets such a bad name in our culture. It is as though we have a built-in bias that whining and a life of nonstop victimhood are somehow intrinsically connected and that's simply not true. What is true is that some people who are deeply devoted to hanging on to a victim identity do an immense amount of whining towards anyone that might be within earshot as a way to justify and prove how unfixable their predicament is in their eyes.

If we extrapolate from those individuals we might incorrectly assume that the whining leads to a victim stance towards life, rather than see whining as a temporary state that some people get stuck in. Whining is a very useful and appropriate stage to go through in the process of moving toward creating the life you really want and many people lose out on the valuable benefits that whining can provide because they are fearful of not being able to stop once they start or that they will alienate others.

So how can you make whining work for you to help you create the life you want? I'm going to teach you a three-step process that you can use to help yourself move along the path to having the

Peeling the Onion

life you want. First of all, start with a basic question: What are you passionately sick of having or not having, experiencing or not experiencing? Let yourself get really clear about your answer and then you're ready to launch into step 1: Name it.

Name everything you are sick of, why you are sick of it, all the ways you are sick of it, how long you have been sick of it, and why you are sick of being sick of those things. Let yourself really feel this—feel your restlessness, your crabbiness, your anger, your upset and your insistence that you deserve better than that. Let yourself feel your dissatisfaction as deeply as you can, all the way down to your bone marrow. The reason you want to do this is because dissatisfaction almost always comes before making the change that leads us to creating true satisfaction.

Okay, so once you are absolutely dissatisfied, what do you do next? At this point, you put step 2 into action: Blame it. During this stage you look for anyone and anything other than yourself to blame for what you are sick of—all of the way from the hugest responsibility possible to the most microscopic involvement imaginable. This is not the time to censor yourself or try to be accountable because we will address that later in step 3.

For now, I want you to have a colossal brainstorm of blaming—unfurl your list of possible sources of blame. The one stipulation is that you either do this process in writing and keep it to yourself or that you find a supportive person who is willing to be an attentive sounding board and who has read these pages and understands the importance of not shaping or limiting your process.

With either one of those options in place, I want you then to just go for it—have a rip-roaring, full-force blame-fest. Let loose with all of the most absurd as well as most accurate blame you can

Name it, Blame it, and Claim it

think of—everything from the profound blame of who abused you as a child to the wonderfully wacky blame that your cat looked at you the wrong way this morning (which happens all the time at my house) and how that started a day full of crazy events.

Now you might be asking, isn't all of this blame counterproductive, and doesn't it just get us off track from accepting accountability and getting on with creating the life we want? That would be absolutely correct if we stopped right there and stayed on the gerbil wheel of blame, going in nonstop verbal circles of who or what did us wrong and how our lives don't work because of it.

Do you want to know the reason why most of us get worried that we will dead end in a cul-de-sac of blame? It's because we have never been given permission, much less encouraged to have an all out blame-fest so we can discharge every ounce of blame until we are totally exhausted and have dug so deep inside that we can no longer find even the smallest piece of blame left within us. One of the best things about this experience is that like many other emotional experiences, we discover that any of our emotional states have a beginning, middle and an end and we start to trust ourselves and our ability to do what we need to do until the feelings pass.

It's a normal function of human nature to look for a cause outside of ourselves for what we do not like, and then to attach blame to that source. By allowing ourselves to have a blame-fest, trusting that we can dive deeply and intensely into that experience and still emerge on the other side clear-headed and functional, we actually then free up our energy for future problem solving because we have indulged our reasonable need to engage in yeah buts—"Yeah, but if he had only" or "Yeah, but no one told me," and we

Peeling the Onion

will no longer feel the need to struggle with that as we move toward dealing with what we don't like about our lives.

This brings us to step 3: Claim it. So we have named what we are deeply sick of and we have had a magnificent blame-fest attributing responsibility to everything outside of ourselves. Now, this next step might surprise you. I absolutely don't care if you ever explore what your role might have been in creating or sustaining whatever it is that you are sick of in your life. I don't care if you take any responsibility for how you got to where you are, although that might be useful to explore if you are at all invested in trying to prevent it from occurring again.

What I do care about is that you take full responsibility for changing what you are sick of—that you get active and assertive in taking steps to make your life different. Claim your responsibility, your intention and your ability to take action to change the things that you are sick of having in your life. When you wait for people and circumstances to change it is like saying that you don't have the power to impact your life in important ways.

Here's an example: Imagine that while at work a package is dropped off for you in the office while you are at lunch. It is an enormous box, much bigger and heavier than anything you could lift with your arms. Upon opening it, you discover that it contains an alarmingly large amount of quickly thawing mackerel. The stench factor is rapidly increasing in your office. What do you do?

If you are in the blame mode, you look for whose fault it is— the delivery company, the person who packed the fish, the person in your office who signed for it—and as momentarily satisfying as this may be, ultimately it doesn't change anything until you acknowledge that even though you in no way feel you created the

Name it, Blame it, and Claim it

problem, it is *you* and precisely you who are facing the unappealing fact of a ton of stinky fish in your office. Once you claim it as your problem you then are in touch with the actual reality, which is that you have an office full of quickly spoiling fish and that it doesn't sit well with you. As soon as you fully acknowledge the reality you are facing, you are on your way to a solution that will better meet your needs because you are dealing with the fact that something needs to change and are taking action by claiming that you see the problem, experience it as a true problem and that you see the need for change.

At the same time, claiming it as a problem and claiming the need for change doesn't mean that you get exactly what you want from a particular person or experience. If what you want out of life is a loving partner and your current partner is not interested in giving that in the way you want and need, your partner is not preventing you from having what you want—only your insistence that you have that experience from that exact person prevents you from having what you want. Sometimes it is necessary to let go of the specifics of what you want (this person, this experience, this timing of it) in order to get the larger, ongoing, satisfying experience of what you desire in your daily life.

As hard as this may be to do in a given moment, it is even more difficult to try to motivate someone to change who has no interest in doing so. Claiming it means that you claim your awareness and understanding of the fact that you have two choices when faced with something that you are sick of—either make a change in your situation or change your attitude and find a different way to view and experience what you previously were sick of having in your life. This may mean looking for hidden benefits in what you disliked or

Peeling the Onion

finding new ways to grow from challenging circumstances or just accepting that you're just not quite ready to make a big change and that you are working towards it.

Anything is okay as long as you claim the fact that this is your life and that you have the right, the ability and the power to let go of what doesn't work for you and to begin to create what does work for you. Name what doesn't work for you, blame the entire universe for it, and then claim the wisdom, power and grace to go change it. You've got what it takes: Name it, blame it, and claim it.

Note to myself:

What behaviors, thoughts and feelings am I willing to peel away and let go of to be my most flourishing self?

CHAPTER 9

The Solution is in the Middle

One of the things that I find most intriguing about human nature is our habitual impulse to continually revert to black and white thinking during times of stress and upheaval. No matter how balanced we normally are personally and professionally, no matter how much reading, therapy or training we've done to learn how to remain open and appropriately responsive during challenging circumstances, it often seems as though that awareness and those skills vanish when we are faced with significant emotional pain. Nowhere is this truer than in the arena of intimate relationships. Time and time again, I watch otherwise intelligent, resilient individuals lurch from one bad black-and-white choice to another, bewildered as to why nothing seems to fully alleviate the pain or generate the results that they truly want.

The difficulty lies in the fact that black-and-white, either/or reactions never really seem to get at the heart of what truly needs to be solved. The solution to a challenging dilemma rarely is to do the direct opposite of what previously didn't work. More often than

Peeling the Onion

not, doing so simply produces the flip side of the same problem with the desired solution still out of reach.

Here's an example: Suppose Trish has a history of choosing partners who are always too busy to give her an appropriate amount of attention, emotional energy and basic connection. Her assessment of what has gone wrong is that all of these partners were too into their careers, workaholics who had no time for emotions or for spending time with her. So, she sets her jaw and determinedly vows to look this time for a partner who just sees a job as something you do to pay the bills and voluntarily shares feelings and emotions with Trish.

So what's wrong with this approach? First of all, while it's understandable that she might logically see this as the solution to her previous problem, it mistakenly assumes that an intense involvement with a career prevents the person from also having a powerful personal relationship and that's not accurate. Second, because she is so focused on finding the opposite of what she perceives has hurt her, she (in classic black-and-white thinking) launches herself on a mission to find exactly the opposite of what hurt her.

Third, this approach sets her up for the opposite set of problems: Instead of having a partner who spends too much time on work, Trish may end up with a partner who fails to think about career concerns and therefore misses out on advancement opportunities or cannot maintain a healthy focus on a relationship with Trish because of being entangled in addictions, infidelity, depression or low self-esteem. Trish, in her search for a partner who volunteers feelings openly, could end up with someone who can never

The Solution is in the Middle

adaptively compartmentalize feelings, who inappropriately and over-indulgently blurts or vents every microscopic emotion regardless of the impact on Trish.

Looking for the opposite of what didn't work previously usually just produces another extreme which doesn't work any better than what came before it. The way to step out of the no-win dilemma of black-and-white thinking is to consider what other options might exist besides the two opposing extremes.

One of the hard truths that I took a long time to learn was that the way to the peace and balance that I was always seeking usually fell somewhere in the middle of the two extremes that I was struggling with and that it offered a much more satisfying option. In Trish's case, that means she doesn't resign herself to highly responsible, over-achieving workaholics with no time for her or settle for floundering, unfocused go-with-the-flow types who have plenty of time for her but bring with them a life that is perpetually in crisis.

The truth is that the solution that will feel the most satisfying generally lies in the middle. For Trish, this might consist of her looking for a partner who shares her work interests so that they can connect around work activities. Or it might mean finding a partner who, when kindly asked to put aside work for some interpersonal connection, can see letting go of work concerns as a request that is positive, helpful and a good reminder to practice life balancing skills with Trish.

When I feel most stuck, it's usually because both of the alternatives to my dilemma seem intolerable, and I feel trapped between two undesirable choices. It is here that I ask myself: "What's the third choice? What's the choice in the middle that I am not seeing or

Peeling the Onion

imagining?" The great news is that it's precisely that middle choice that often holds the keys to a new experience. You can do this. Find your solution, the one that truly works, right in the middle.

Note to myself:

What behaviors, thoughts and feelings am I willing to peel away and let go of to be my most flourishing self?

CHAPTER 8

Stop Trying to Make Others Stay

In my twenties, I spent much of my energy trying to get men who did not want to stay, to stay—to not leave emotionally, whether through their chaos and emotional deadness, through their mental illness and anger, or through their emotional and sexual infidelities. I tried to get them to not leave through their indifference, through their weakness and arrogance, to not leave through their self-deception and shallowness, to not leave through their simple lack of desire and valuing of me.

I believed that if I could keep them from leaving that I could keep the love from leaving, without ever realizing that the love was never fully there. I was so focused on keeping the love from leaving that I failed to notice that it never arrived in the first place. I was so dedicated to keeping the love from leaving that I failed to dedicate myself to the one thing that could save me: Me. I made a religion, a profession out of willing men to stay, of trying to will my self-worth into their eyes.

I abandoned myself over and over again while I tried to convince yet another man not to do what I already had done to myself—leave

Peeling the Onion

me in the lurch. Until a man could choose me with conviction, certainty, unending loyalty and unwavering attention, I could not embrace myself with those same attributes that I so desperately wanted to receive. I was willing to give up everything to not be given up, when instead I could have gained real love, self-love by simply giving up, by letting those who wanted to go simply go.

I was waiting for someone to stay and love me so I could get started living my life—to have a chance to find all the untouched, untapped areas of my creativity, passion and purpose that I somehow never got to in all of my waiting for love to choose me and finally stay. What I failed to realize was that people who don't love you are supposed to leave in order to make room for those who do love you and who will stay. I wish I had known back then that I should have been glad I lost, and glad that I did not win what was not good for me. Looking back, I am grateful for everything that was withheld from me that made a life with that person impossible, because it actually saved me from entering into a life deeply lacking in love and aliveness.

The withholding of love that I battled so strongly against in my twenties actually protected me from a life that would have killed off the very best in me, that would have left me feeling perpetually off balance, trying to prove my worth, struggling to not be left, to not be discarded and in doing that I would have ultimately discarded my light and all that I was meant to be. The lack of love that I felt such pain over ironically created the opportunity to stay true to myself, to the very love and life I sought, to stay open to myself and my experiences and to feel the wonder and delight of me rather than wait for someone to notice and name it for me.

Stop Trying to Make Others Stay

I've learned so much since then: Trying to will others to stay is not a terribly powerful position to occupy in a relationship, and who *really* wants to know that you managed to make someone stay who in no way wanted to stay? And how on earth would you make that happen? Guilt? Obligation? Fear? Intimidation? Who truly wants a relationship created by those means?

Finally I realized that I did not want to be desired by someone who cannot value love, who does not know how to love, who battles connection yet fears abandonment. And even more importantly, I realized that in my pursuit to get others to stay, I had absolutely missed the entire point: It is their job to know how to stay. It is their job to figure out why the relationship matters, what there is about me that is worth cherishing and celebrating, why they should continue to seek me out, continue to like me, long for me, love me.

So what does this all mean? Primarily, it means that you stand tall and strong within yourself and remember the wisdom of calmly letting others come and go. It also means realizing that if you simply let people change their minds, let them pull their love away and leave you, hard and hurtful as it may be, all you are then left with is love. All that remains is real love, love rooted in deep choice and solid desire and that the unwavering love you desire has been there all along, right inside of you. And if you notice it, name it and cherish it, the burning need to have someone else do it begins to fall away because now you know it's true and that you no longer need to prove your worth.

Commit to your lovability and let those who cannot happily and wholeheartedly join you, leave as soon as they can. Be brave.

Peeling the Onion

Trust that love will come. Fight the urge to close your heart, and leave the space wide open for someone thrilled to love you enthusiastically and wonderfully well.

Note to myself:

What behaviors, thoughts and feelings am I willing to peel away and let go of to be my most flourishing self:

CHAPTER 7

Suspect the Best

It is really difficult sometimes to think the best about others, especially when you are unclear about someone's behaviors, motives and intentions toward you. There seems to be a gravitational pull towards viewing the other person through wary, suspicious eyes, trying to determine who's out to get you, who really just cares about themselves, who's going to burn you or betray you.

It is also incredibly hard to suspect the best if you've been through a series of life experiences that have demonstrated just how unbelievably dreadful other people can behave when you've openly given them your trust and belief in them. It's not unusual to feel misled and mistreated by people you chose to put your faith and hope in, only to ultimately be let down or betrayed by them.

Unfortunately, usually what happens after people feel their trust has been misplaced is that they think that they trusted the wrong thing, not simply the wrong person. They think they blew it by trusting or believing that good things were possible, that they could rely on what someone told them, that they believed that they could have what they wanted. They vow to never be so blind and stupid

Peeling the Onion

again, to keep their wits about them, to stay skeptical, to believe it only if and when they see it.

What they don't realize is that they were absolutely right to believe that good things are possible, they were right to rely on what someone said and they were right to believe that they could have what they wanted. Even if one person or a series of people mislead, disappoint or betray them, it is still right, smart and strong to suspect the best about people and what is possible.

The point is nothing is gained by suspecting the worst; nothing valuable is protected by doing it that couldn't be protected by using good common sense from a more open and optimistic viewpoint. In other words, don't hand over your debit card, the most vulnerable secrets from your past or anything else that would leave you reeling if the person turned out to be untrustworthy.

When you suspect the worst, you miss out on all kinds of lovely energy and effort from people because they eventually become discouraged and uninspired to give you their best when they are perpetually scrutinized with suspicion and therefore essentially blamed for things that they may never have considered doing to you or to anyone else. The irony is that as you withhold your positive belief in others, the people most likely to leave will be the healthy individuals who know that proving themselves is unnecessary and that dealing with literal and implied accusations is not a good use of their life force.

The really big users, the big time takers will just invest a bit more energy into eventually wearing down your defenses and winning you over. When that happens you may, like many others, decide that where you blew it was that you gave in too soon and that next time you will wait even longer before you trust someone. Great

Suspect the Best

strategy, except it doesn't work. The truth is there will always be people who fail to treat us lovingly and well. If being suspicious and wary kept them at bay, then there might be a valid point for living that way, but it doesn't keep them at bay.

And even more importantly, suspecting the best about others doesn't mean that you are stupid or blind to the fact that some people deliberately choose to be dishonest in their interactions with others. Those people will always exist and you'll always figure out who they are when they tip enough of their cards. Suspecting the best won't allow them to get away with more, in fact it'll probably increase their guilt and discomfort, causing them to leave sooner rather than later.

Suspecting the best will, on the other hand, sometimes encourage others to strive for a deeper level of good intentions and positive behaviors because your attitude of suspecting the best implies that you see who they can be at their very best. It's almost as though you offer out the approval and appreciation first and then they have the opportunity to show up with the best of themselves. One of the greatest things about suspecting the best is that you give others the chance to prove you right over and over again in all kinds of wonderful ways and who wouldn't want to do that? You can do it. Suspect the best.

Peeling the Onion

Note to myself:

What behaviors, thoughts and feelings am I willing to peel away and let go of to be my most flourishing self?

CHAPTER 6

Four Steps to Making Your Dreams Come True

There are four simple steps to make your dreams come true:
1. See More
2. Want More
3. Feel More
4. Be More

The first step, See More, means that for a treasured dream to stand a chance to come true, it's absolutely essential that you expand your vision of what's possible. This means that you not only see the big picture, but that you see a potentially even bigger picture of what else might be possible that you have not previously considered. You might ask yourself, "What haven't I let myself imagine that I could achieve, have or experience?" What things have I already decided that I cannot do and why? What might I not be paying attention to that might prove that my limited beliefs are wrong?

It could also mean asking trusted others what other possibilities they see that you may not be aware of—what areas of your life and your talents do they see you capable of expanding and expressing?

Peeling the Onion

Seeing more also means seeing and believing that your life can be better than it is, that you can have a deeper, richer, fuller experience of what matters most and what you truly long and hunger to have in your life.

It is precisely that longing and hungering that leads to the second step, Want More. Here your task is to let yourself actually want the healthy things that you want, crave the healthy things that you crave, miss what you've been missing. It means not feeling afraid or ashamed of your appetite—that you let your appetite be big, bold—that you acknowledge your hunger to take up space, make an impact, inspire someone, shape your life, create change and ask for what you want exactly how and when you want it.

Wanting more is healthy, it tells us what we desire, what we are drawn to, where to direct our energies, where we are not yet satisfied. And guess what happens when you get clear about what you truly want? Well, for one thing, all that permission to want what you want leads to you feeling your hunger for what you want, which leads you to the third step, Feel More.

A crucial part of having your dreams come true means being willing to feel whatever you need to feel in order to have those dreams unfold. This means being willing not only to feel the feelings that you feel comfortable and at home with, but also being willing to experience feelings that are unfamiliar, out of your comfort zone, and perhaps out of proportion to what you usually allow yourself.

It means that you let yourself feel passionate, intense, grandiose, silly, expansive, confused, fearful, angry, lost, confident, joyful, hopeful—that you let yourself have the direct experience of your feelings without censoring or judging them—that you welcome them as important clues and input to assist you in clarifying and

Four Steps to Making Your Dreams Come True

continuing to move toward your dreams. It means not declaring any feeling off-limits because whatever you feel the impulse to avoid is probably something that will be an essential factor in achieving your dreams.

When you allow yourself the experience of fully feeling whatever emotion that pursuing your dreams conjures up, you are already putting the fourth step, Be More, into place. Be More essentially means that you cast aside whatever limiting beliefs you and others have had about what you can and cannot be and, instead of working hard to believe that more is possible, you take the same energy you'd put into trying to change your beliefs into actually becoming what you truly want to be.

You stop wondering if you can be more, wondering when you can be more, how'll you'll be more and you just get busy becoming more—you put yourself in the environments and around the people where this is possible. You stop waiting for the security, sunshine and serenity you need to blossom and you just make the decision to start the process of blossoming right now. You decide that it's time to do it and it has been for a long time. So get going with the *be-ing* of being the person you long to be and start having the dreams you've always desired finally start to come true. You're long overdue. See More. Want More. Feel More. Be More. Make your dreams come true.

Peeling the Onion

Note to myself:

What behaviors, thoughts and feelings am I willing to peel away to be my most flourishing self?

CHAPTER 5

Stop Waiting to Feel Motivated

It's difficult to make positive changes, especially in regards to long-standing health- related habits like exercise and food intake. There is so much useful, accurate information available yet many women still struggle with weight and fitness issues. Why?

Often when I ask women that question, their response is that they couldn't find the motivation to begin, or upon beginning, they soon lost the motivation to continue with their new habits. Motivation then becomes a mark or measure of how serious you are, how much will or determination you have, how strong you are and how successful you are or aren't at achieving your goals.

Motivation is then seen as a positive character attribute, and lack of motivation is seen as a flaw akin to laziness or self-indulgence. Falling into this black-and-white, either/or thinking does women a terrible disservice, because they spend endless hours beating themselves up over their inability to unearth the determination to regularly engage in the activities that would improve their physical well-being.

Peeling the Onion

While motivation works wonderfully well for some women, the truth is most women will never truly find the steady motivation to engage in healthy eating and exercising behaviors in an ongoing, consistent way. If you're like most women, this approach will never work. Personally, I've tried everything I can think of to make it work for myself but I always end up back in the same place—feeling absolutely no motivation to get up at 6:00 a.m. to go out for a run in the cold, dark, rainy Oregon weather in search of better cardiovascular health and lower body fat. I'd always rather stay cocooned in bed for an hour longer with the cats slumbering on top of me. And as cozy as that may be, it certainly doesn't move me any closer to achieving my health goals.

So what's the solution? Simply this: Stop waiting to feel motivated. Save all the time and energy that goes into trying to force yourself to feel motivated or trying to wait for the right amount of motivation to emerge before you tackle your goals because this approach rarely works.

I remember making long lists of how I would benefit from better fitness and nutrition. And while those lists were intellectually compelling they never really grabbed me emotionally. Finally, a light bulb went off for me. What if I just engaged in those healthy fitness and eating behaviors whether I felt like it or not—in the same way that I did many other necessary life behaviors without searching for powerful tactics to motivate me?

I started by reminding myself that I never feel motivated to floss my teeth or take out the trash or clean the cat box, I just do it because it's a part of the daily maintenance of life. I don't spend time running down a list of all the vital ways flossing contributes to good dental health or how regular removal of trash cuts down on

Stop Waiting to Feel Motivated

disease, odor and an influx of bugs and rodents. I do it because it's simpler just to take out the trash than to think about it.

I applied a similar tactic to the issue of exercise. I stopped trying to convince myself of all of the positive reasons why I should exercise, and stopped frightening myself with all the negative outcomes if I failed to exercise. Instead I realized that just as I was probably never going to say, "Woo-hoo, I get to floss my teeth and I love it," I was probably never going to feel thrilled about working out.

I started telling myself, "I know you don't want to do this. I don't blame you, it's dark and cold but we're doing this anyway—it is just part of what happens in the morning." I'd like to say I discovered the joys of exercise and that endorphins motivated me to continue my new behaviors happily and effortlessly, but that never happened. It's as though every morning I have amnesia because there's never been a morning when I wouldn't rather remain in bed. What has changed is that I stopped waiting for the desire and drive to work out and simply viewed working out as one of the basic details of my daily life—just like commuting in traffic, feeding the cats, and paying bills. When I stopped waiting to feel like I wanted to do it and simply just did it, I was suddenly working out regularly.

Give yourself permission to complain and feel absolutely uninspired and then just shrug your shoulders and simply take action. It's amazing how much easier it is to just decide that you're going to exercise rather than trying to conjure up exactly the right emotional state to feel inspired to take action. One of the great payoffs of this approach is that your health will improve without you ever needing to find or maintain even an ounce of motivation. Give it a try. Just decide.

Peeling the Onion

Note to myself:

What behaviors, thoughts and feelings am I willing to peel away and let go of to be my most flourishing self?

CHAPTER 4

Claim Your Baggage

Would you like to see more peace in the world and less pain and heartache? Do you want a simple, straightforward way to put that creation in motion right this minute? The best way each of us can contribute to the presence of peaceful, healing energy in the world is to truly know ourselves, which means to know our strengths and gifts as well as our wounds and where we are still lost and confused.

The most dangerous person in the world is the person who announces himself or herself totally healed, totally lacking in any unresolved issues and if you hear someone say this run away as fast as you can. There are several reasons why it is important to leave these individuals. First, anyone highly evolved enough to have this potentially be true would not feel the need to proclaim it, rather they'd simply be living it without the need to have others notice and give them credit for it.

Second, people who trumpet that they are absolutely free of personal issues are sure to happily point out the array of issues that you have yet to master, but they thankfully mastered *years* ago. You may find that issues that never belonged to you are suddenly

Peeling the Onion

deemed central to who you are and how you function. The difficulty of being with someone who is afraid or unwilling to know themselves and face the truth of who they are is that you end up being accused of all the aspects that they are attempting to run from and disown.

This would simply be annoying except that enormous confusion can set in when issues that are not yours are continually attributed to you, and even though it doesn't feel true, whom are you supposed to believe? Maybe it doesn't seem true because it *is* your issue and you're just in denial. Perhaps though it has nothing to do with you and then suddenly you find yourself sorting through confusion that was never yours to begin with, confusion that belongs to someone else. This is one of the biggest causes of chaos and pain—people who are unaware of their old wounds and blow the shrapnel of their anger and anxiety everywhere.

Their wounds create pain, but because they are in denial about their wounds, they cannot focus on getting to the source of their wounds and then healing and freeing themselves of their pain. Instead, since they perceive themselves as fully together, any pain they feel must be coming from you and the mess that you embody. They focus on trying to help you be less of a loser (and you may have never thought you were one until you met them), but since you were never the cause of their pain you can never alleviate it and so the cycle of pain, confusion and heartache continues.

Do you see why it is so vital that each of us can clearly and honestly express, "This is what I am still working on," "These are the difficult and jerky ways I sometimes behave and they have nothing to do with you?" When you truly know yourself and can give accurate and useful information about the best and most

Claim Your Baggage

challenging parts of yourself you protect others from the more disruptive and disharmonious parts of your growth process.

Part of loving others well is making certain that they do not become the dumping ground for all the parts of yourself that you'd rather not deal with because even if you manage to successfully scoot away from dealing with your issues, everyone around you will be dealing with them two-fold. They'll reap the unfortunate impact of your unexplored reactive defenses to your pain as well as facing the thankless task of trying to talk to you about the parts of yourself that you refuse to take ownership of and be accountable for exploring, understanding and changing in healthy ways.

Have you ever spent time around someone who is always right? Did you notice that they usually have someone around them who is always wrong? In a similar way, if you have no issues, no areas in which you are striving to grow then someone very close to you will get the unenviable role of the messed up, sick, dysfunctional basket case. If you want healthy, balanced relationships, it's vital that you claim half of the baggage and that you carry your own bags. It is deeply unfair to expect someone you love to lug around the heavy baggage that you acquired long before you ever met them.

Lighten everyone's load and everyone's spirit—carry your own bags as you move through your life. Hang on to what is valuable and what works for you and leave the rest behind.

Peeling the Onion

Note to myself:

What behaviors, thoughts and feelings am I willing to peel away and let go of to be my most flourishing self?

Chapter 3

Trying to Outrun Pain

One of my biggest pet peeves about our society is that it encourages and teaches people to outrun and dodge their pain. Ironically, this belief that it is both possible and desirable to perpetually avoid painful feelings is one of the main causes of so much avoidable chaos and heartache.

So much of what mass media promotes is the notion that if we look the right way, have the right things, seek the right experiences or improve ourselves in the right ways that we will get to have a life full of pleasure. Implied within this perspective is that pain is for losers, for people not savvy enough to figure out what they need to do differently to make the pain go away.

So people turn to whatever they can to try to make the pain disappear—constant activity with no chance to sit still, rescuing everyone around them, alcohol, drugs, an unrelenting focus on work, getting lost in food, shopping, relationships—anything that creates external chaos and keeps the focus and energy on dealing with that chaos rather than facing the internal feelings of pain.

Peeling the Onion

A large part of why this occurs is the fact that so few of us have had the experience of truly having been comforted when we felt pain—we have lacked having someone fully present who keeps us company while we sit and feel our pain without trying to reshape our experiences for us. When someone is able to be there when we are hurt and afraid and they allow us the time and space to talk, flounder, cry and sort our way through it we learn two very important things.

One is that we don't disappear or disintegrate when we feel our pain because we are held in the loving gaze of another person who truly sees and accepts us no matter how messy and scary our feelings. Two, we are able to discover that when we sit still and actually allow ourselves to have our painful feelings, we learn that like any other experience, feeling our pain has a beginning, middle and end to it.

Often we terrorize ourselves with the faulty belief that if we start to feel the things that hurt us there will be no end to our pain and no way to shut it off once we start. One of the main reasons that we buy into this belief is that upon the rare occasion that we are not able to keep the pain at bay it does swamp us because we've stomped so much down inside of us. Furthermore, we suck at dealing with it because we almost never get any practice at it and you only get good at what you practice.

The image I like to use to convey this point concerns going to the dentist. Some people are terrified of going to the dentist and will do whatever they can within their power to avoid it. Because of this, they may inevitably try not to focus on anything to do with dental care, dodging visits for cleaning, being haphazard about flossing and brushing less than thoroughly.

Trying to Outrun Pain

And guess what happens? Unlike people who regularly visit the dentist and generally have brief uneventful visits, the people who avoid the dentist usually end up there, having increased the likelihood through their avoidance that their experiences may be both lengthy and painful, thus reinforcing their original faulty belief about avoiding the dentist.

This same principle can be applied to the emotional aspects of our lives—whatever we try to consistently avoid will eventually create shrieking, unavoidable pain that we cannot ignore and will at that point be so unpleasant and difficult to deal with that we will convince ourselves that we were right to avoid dealing with it in the first place.

The fact of the matter is that there is no escape from feeling your pain. You may be able to delay it for a time but eventually you'll end up experiencing it because something will happen that makes it impossible to outrun your pain. You or someone you love will get sick, financial setbacks will occur, relationships will change or end, you'll fail at achieving some important goal, old ways of coping won't work at all anymore.

In that moment, if you're lucky (or maybe just too exhausted) perhaps you'll see that no matter what you do you don't get to dodge feeling pain and loss. And if you're really lucky, you'll get the idea to let yourself feel just a little bit of your old pain every day until you've caught up and all you have to do is deal with your current pain as it arises in your life.

Because the truth is that other cultures figured this out long before us—that if you sit still, breathe in and honor your painful feelings by simply noticing them, not judging them or pushing them away they pass away like any other feeling—like hunger,

Peeling the Onion

silliness or curiosity. Every emotion is always in movement and it is only when we try to hold things down and deny them that we hurt ourselves.

Hard as we may try, it's simply impossible to outrun our pain. It will ultimately catch up with us. And do you know what's even worse? While we're spending all that misdirected and wasted energy trying to outrun our pain, do you know what we unwittingly do instead? We outrun joy. We are so focused on not feeling our pain that we fail to sit still, open our hearts and our awareness to what is in front of us, within us and instead we end up outrunning the immense joy that is possible for us.

You can't outrun pain. You can only outrun joy. So stand still, feel whatever is true for you. Remember that it has a beginning, middle and an end. You are bigger and stronger than any of your feelings. You can do this. Let the joy catch up with you.

Note to myself:

What behaviors, thoughts and feelings am I willing to peel away and let go of to be my most flourishing self?

CHAPTER 2

Trouble Saying No

For years I had an incredibly difficult time saying no. For one thing, just the sound of the word bothered me—short, abrupt, harsh and well, so **final**. To complicate matters further, I could always find reasons why the request that was being made was a reasonable thing for the other person to want and the simple fact that I didn't want to do it always seemed petty and selfish. After all, how dare I say no when I was capable of doing it?

At the very bottom of my struggle to say no was my deeply ingrained belief that saying no was mean—absolutely lacking in compassion, generosity and kindness. In my mind, being a kind and loving person meant saying yes even when I didn't feel like it, which was a lot of the time. And being a kind, loving person who felt she had to say yes soon turned me into a person who was absolutely exhausted by meeting everyone else's wants and needs and who had totally lost track of her own.

The turning point for me was when a friend gently remarked that perhaps saying yes when I meant no and was feeling secretly resentful and burnt out might *appear* loving but in truth wasn't

Peeling the Onion

I only focused on looking loving rather than truly *being* loving? Ouch. And incredibly accurate.

Armed with an entirely different perspective, I soon grasped that the genuinely kind and loving thing might be to say no to someone's request of me. Finally feeling willing to consider this I started to explore ways to increase my comfort and ability to say no.

Guess what? Nothing really worked, that is, very well or for very long. Certainly I gathered useful information on how to communicate well, how to be assertive, use "I" messages, prioritize wants, negotiate competing preferences and make healthy compromises.

But the truth is, most of the time I found myself reverting to my habitual response—saying yes with my mouth when my gut was screaming no. If ignorance is bliss, then self-awareness without the ability to take action on it is pure torment. And that's how it felt, painful, confusing and somewhat hopeless that I'd ever be able to truly change that part of my life.

Finally, I let myself really breathe in the full truth—I just hated the idea of saying no—even though it might be the most real and honest thing I could say in a given moment. I still hated saying it and it still felt mean.

As I continued to explore where that belief had sprung from, I realized that many of my childhood experiences consisted of being on the receiving end of so many heartless and calculatingly withholding, deliberately unnecessary experiences of someone saying no when they easily could have said yes. Those experiences left me feeling the harshness and intended cruelty and with a child's logic and a child's need to see love even where it ceased to exist, I believed it was the saying of no that was cruel and unloving rather than seeing that the cruelty and lack of care came from the spirit of the person saying the word, not the word itself. And I also realized that part of saying yes so much was my attempt to undo the hurt and pain of my childhood by turning every hurtful no into a helpful yes.

Okay, so great clarity but still no plan. I realized that while I still wasn't able to say no directly I didn't want to say anything like "maybe" or "let me think about it and get back to you" because I would spend the time between saying those two statements and possibly saying no agonizing about it. What I needed instead was a simple way to interrupt my knee-jerk habit of saying yes that would give me a chance to take a breath and say no.

What I finally hit on was to say no backwards—to simply say "on" when I felt like saying no. When a friend asked me if I wanted to do an activity that I had no desire to do, I looked at her and said "on." As you might expect, she said "What?" Then, with a big smile and a laugh, I said, "Whoops, I'm trying to practice saying no and sometimes it just comes out backwards, so thanks for asking but I'd rather not."

And amazement of amazements, it worked. Most people found my approach to saying no so silly (or maybe so lame) that it rarely occurred to them to argue with me. More importantly, since I was usually laughing during some part of the exchange the issue of feeling mean quickly faded away. And here's the best part: The more I practiced saying no, the more I got to express and say yes to the true me.

Peeling the Onion

Note to myself:

What behaviors, thoughts and feelings am I willing to peel away and let go of to be my most flourishing self?

CHAPTER 1

Fear Less Love More

One crucial way to become more of who you were always meant to be is to stop focusing your energy on fending off what you fear and turn your attention to welcoming more of what you love into your life. Most of us are highly aware that we have a limited amount of energy to expend during any given day. Where does your energy go? Are you braced against adversity, on the lookout for what could go wrong, for who might disappoint or betray you? How does that shape the tone and feel of your day?

Instead of focusing on what could go wrong imagine moving through your day looking for and taking note of every interaction and experience that creates pleasure for you. Try to picture yourself moving from acknowledgement and experience of something you enjoy to another enjoyable experience and onto yet another one. What feelings arise for you when you attempt to imagine this?

While it is certainly important to not walk through the world blindly unaware of potential harm and danger, many of us have honed our ability to scan our environment and those who inhabit it for even the slightest flicker of possible danger that we have

Peeling the Onion

severely diminished our capacity to find pleasure and delight in our daily experiences.

Delight. When was the last time you truly felt delight? What would it be like to fully experience that and then ask yourself, "How do I welcome more delight into my life?" What would it be like to place a big welcome mat and a wide open door in front of the things you love?

So how do you do that? First and foremost, you stop doing the things you are afraid to stop doing just because you think doing them will keep you safe from what you fear. Make a list of all the things that you do out of fear. Which ones are not essential to you living within the legal constraints of your community or within the boundaries of your personal values? Can you see how much of your energy goes into fearful thoughts of "I should" or "I have to?" What if you directed that same energy toward creating more of what you love?

Here's an example: Jen spends much of her life force trying to make sure that Rob doesn't stop loving her. She has spent the past five years of their relationship trying to fend off any perception that Rob might not be madly in love with her. She is continually fearful that he may be losing interest in her and in her fear she constricts, feels timid, closes down her energy and consequently becomes less interesting. In an attempt to ward off what she fears she has in effect created exactly what she was trying to avoid. What if instead she had focused on welcoming more of what she loves into her life? What might she do differently?

If being afraid and going through life fearing loss made people's lives better I'd be all for it. I'd be arguing the merits of it and teaching people more efficient ways to build that into their daily lives. But the truth is, fear is a spirit killer—it robs people of passion, of power, of potential.

And while I'd be the first to assert the importance of taking a proactive and preventative approach to certain aspects of life, too much focus on fending off what could go wrong leaves little energy left over to create a life that goes right. No matter how careful you are some bad things will happen. No matter how tightly boarded up you keep your life, certain negative experiences will find a way to break in, no matter how carefully guarded you are or how hard you try to prevent it. The only thing you will manage to keep at bay are the things that could give you the most delight, because you'll be too worn out being afraid to hear the joy and aliveness knocking at your door.

Open up your heart and invite what you love in—make room for it, make time for it, save energy to cherish it. The more your life is filled with the things you love the less room there is for fear. Although you could argue that the more you love the more there is to lose, what's the alternative? It's like saying that you're only going to have one friend rather than ten because that way if the person dies before you do you'll only miss one person instead of ten. Do you see the crazy logic in this? By trying to ward off future pain and loss what really gets warded off is the chance to utterly go for it—to experience all the love and aliveness that is in front of you every day.

The things you give your attention to become what you are committed to because it's what you give your life force to each day. Break up with your fear. Send it packing. Tell it you know you deserve better. Tell it you want something more. Tell it you can do better. And then do it. Start inviting the things you love back into

Peeling the Onion

your life. Get curious about what brings you joy. Let yourself have what you love.

Note to myself:

What behaviors, thoughts and feelings am I willing to peel away and let go of to be my most flourishing self?

Afterword

This has been the hardest manuscript that I've ever written. Usually I write about topics that I've mostly figured out, but this book began out of my floundering and all the ways that I felt lost from my truest self. The struggle with this manuscript echoed the struggle within myself. What is true for me? What needs to be stripped away? What is preventing a flourishing life from unfolding right now? What is missing and needs to be added so that a flourishing life is truly possible? And most importantly, how willing am I to peel my onion?

More than anything else, this has been a book about willingness—the willingness to let go of the emotions, thoughts and behaviors that never truly were mine, ones I added layer by layer as the years passed, ones I added trying to dodge the inevitable pain, loss and fear that comes with being alive. The irony is that every layer I added to try to protect myself from pain only postponed it and each layer caused me to be less alive, less brave, less clear, less open-hearted and less of my truest self.

So armed with my willingness, a box of tissues for the inevitable tears that come with peeling the onion and fortified by a wonderful array of helpers and healers, I made a pledge to myself and I'd like you to take that pledge with me:

I dare myself to flourish. I want to flourish as much as I possibly can, in ways that allow all of us a chance to truly flourish—not just

Peeling the Onion

my loved ones. I want my community, my country and the entire planet to flourish.

I know that all kinds of people may disrupt my authentic flourishing, interrupt my most revitalizing pursuits, tell me that my flourishing nature is selfish, too outrageous, too unsettling, too inconvenient to fit into day-to-day life. I will not believe them.

It is important to flourish. Children need flourishing energy around them, teens need to see adults who are clearly flourishing so that, as teens, they can believe there is a reason to persist through tough times and that becoming an adult is worthwhile and meaningful. I pledge to be a flourishing role model. I will extend my flourishing energy and true enthusiasm for life to create a ripple effect of flourishing. I will remember that when I ask what needs my flourishing focus today, that part of the answer will always include me. I am no longer lost. I am here. I am here to flourish.

So, dear readers, there it is. Thank you for taking this pledge with me. The world needs all of the flourishing energy we can create and with your help we can begin to create a revolution of flourishing, a revolution of authenticity, a revolution of joy.

September 2015

Made in the USA
Las Vegas, NV
05 January 2025